Wakefield Press

HARRY HODGETTS

Raised and educated in Adelaide, John Davis taught History, Australian Studies and Theory of Knowledge at Pembroke School, Kensington Park, and is a life member and a former trustee. He is the author of *Principles and Pragmatism*, a history of Pembroke School and its antecedents – Girton Girls' School and King's College. In retirement, he volunteered at the History Trust of South Australia and at Pembroke School. In 2014, the school published his updated second edition of *Principles and Pragmatism*. When researching the history of Girton in 1989, he first learned of Harry Hodgetts and his intriguing life story.

By the same author

Principles and Pragmatism:
A History of Girton, King's College and Pembroke School (1991)

A Remarkable Match:
A Short History of Pembroke School, 1974–1993 (1994)

Principles & Pragmatism: Volume 1,
A History of Girton and King's College,
the antecedents of Pembroke School (2014)

Principles & Pragmatism: Volume 2,
A History of Pembroke School, 1974–2010 (2014)

Harry Hodgetts

*The flawed broker behind
Don Bradman's move
to Adelaide*

JOHN DAVIS

Wakefield Press
16 Rose Street
Mile End
South Australia 5031
www.wakefieldpress.com.au

First published 2024

Copyright © John Davis, 2024

All rights reserved. This book is copyright. Apart from
any fair dealing for the purposes of private study, research,
criticism or review, as permitted under the Copyright Act,
no part may be reproduced without written permission.
Enquiries should be addressed to the publisher.

Cover design by Michael Deves, Wakefield Press
Edited by Julia Beaven, Wakefield Press
Typeset by Michael Deves, Wakefield Press

ISBN 978 1 92304 226 1

 A catalogue record for this book is available from the National Library of Australia

 Wakefield Press thanks Coriole Vineyards for continued support

  This publication was supported by the History Trust of South Australia's South Australian History Fund

Praise for *Harry Hodgetts*

'*Harry Hodgetts: The flawed broker behind Don Bradman's move to Adelaide* is a detailed, accessible and evocative account of the former leading South Australian stockbroker Harry Hodgetts' rise and fall.'

– Barry Nicholls

'This is an elegant addition to Wakefield Press's history series and in a slim volume John Davis has done a fine job in recreating Hodgetts' social, business and sporting milieu before concluding that he took an unethical, illegal path to trade his way out of trouble when he was hopelessly in debt.'

– Dr Bernard Whimpress

'John Davis has handsomely revealed one of the historical secrets of the city, not without shedding light on other aspects of the Adelaide story. This fulfils neatly a niche in our local history, that will hopefully be duly recognised by the State. It is a valid contribution to this bourgeoning literature, which Wakefield Press increasingly honours with its beautiful books.'

– Dr David Faber

Contents

Introduction		1
Chapter 1	The Making of Harry and Edith Hodgetts	4
Chapter 2	Making Good	13
Chapter 3	A Good Sport, An Outstanding Sports Administrator	29
Chapter 4	Brokering a Deal with Bradman	41
Chapter 5	Service Without Reward	52
Chapter 6	Keeping Up Appearances	70
Chapter 7	The Road to Ruin	80
Chapter 8	Financial Folly and Failure	87
Chapter 9	Public Shame	94
Chapter 10	Fallout	106
Epilogue		120
Notes		125
Acknowledgements		151
Resources		152
Index		157

Introduction

In Adelaide's leafy Holden Street, Kensington Park, there are elegant sandstone villas, a 1960s 'colonial' house, a bungalow, the Girton Campus of Pembroke School and a red-brick, neo-Georgian two-storey house. When Test-cricket matches are played at Adelaide Oval the residents of Holden Street sometimes advise interstate and international visitors that the house they are looking for is the neo-Georgian building. Some of these visitors are fanatics, there to pay homage to 'The Don', their doyen of cricket – for this house was the home of Sir Donald George Bradman.

It is doubtful if any cricketing pilgrims have walked the extra 140 metres along Holden Street and around the corner into Park Road where they could find a grand two-storey villa set on a large suburban block. This was the home of Henry Warburton ('Harry') Hodgetts Jnr, the man behind Bradman's move to Adelaide. Hodgetts' former home is across the road from the Girton Campus of Pembroke School, which was established in 1974 when Girton – a girls' school – and neighbouring boys' school, King's College, merged. Hodgetts educated two daughters at Girton, and Bradman one.[1]

Hodgetts served as chairman of Girton's Board of Directors from 1926 until 1945. Independent Schools recognise stalwart leaders in tangible ways, often by naming a building in their honour. Pembroke does not have a 'Hodgetts Hall', or a 'Hodgetts Library', or 'The Hodgetts Laboratories'. There is nothing that acknowledges his long service to Girton. When he died in 1949, the school did not make a public comment about him. There was one short statement in the minutes of the directors' meeting for 17 October 1949. It stated that Hodgetts was

> a tireless worker in his direction of the school's affairs, and by his repeated generosity, his almost daily visits to the school and his interest in every phase of its activities, he has deserved to go down to memory as one of the most faithful friends of Girton.

Why did the school that Hodgetts supported so generously not celebrate his life? What accounts for this man's fall from grace?

In September 1945, Hodgetts, a sharebroker, pleaded guilty before Justice Frederick Richards in the Criminal Court of South Australia to four charges of fraudulent conversion and one charge of false pretences, together involving about £13,500.[2] On 10 September, Adelaide's evening paper, the *News*, reported that Justice Richards had that afternoon sentenced Hodgetts to five years' gaol on each of the fraud charges and three years on the false pretences charge. The terms were to be served concurrently. In his summing up the judge said that Hodgetts' conduct was 'a severe blow to public confidence generally in men of business'.[3] Hodgetts was incarcerated in Yatala Labour Prison. His public disgrace was complete.

This book explores the rise and fall of Harry Hodgetts, his role in shaping Bradman's career outside of cricket, and the consequences of his crimes. A search of the Australian

Introduction

National Library catalogue for 'Don Bradman' identifies 211 items, including 121 books. Swapping 'Don Bradman' for 'Henry Warburton Hodgetts' draws no response. So much has been said and written about Bradman, but 'Hodgetts' is barely a footnote in the record of the great cricketer's career. While Bradman was the only Australian cricketer to be knighted, the man who was instrumental in his move to Adelaide and who set him on the path to a successful business career was sent to gaol. Hodgetts deserved his fate, but he warrants greater recognition than being consigned to Trotsky's infamous 'dustbin of history'. This book attempts to redress that oversight.

Chapter 1

The Making of Harry and Edith Hodgetts

Henry Warburton Hodgetts Jnr married Mary Edith Gordon Gwynne at St Aidan's Anglican Church, Marden, on Wednesday 16 October 1912. Henry was usually known as 'Harry' and Mary as 'Edith'. Edith's father had died in 1905 and her mother organised the reception at the family's home, Glynde Place, Payneham.[1] Marriage customs aside, Harry's home would not have done: he was living at the Tea Tree Gully Post Office.[2]

The *Chronicle* reported the wedding in its Ladies' Page, with detailed descriptions of the church decorations, the ladies' dresses and the new bride's going-away outfit. The men's dress went unreported. But, when it came to name dropping, Adelaide gentry families invited to the wedding included Belt, Bowman, Levi and Tennant. Despite her grand-sounding name and family links to a former South Australian explorer, Mrs W. Egerton-Warburton failed to make gentry status and was a step below on the social ladder, along with others attending.[3]

Harry was 30 years old, his wife 34. It was unusual for women to marry younger men, and both Harry (1882–1949) and Edith (1878–1953) were older than the median age at which males and females then married. Edith's age at marriage was 10 years above the median for women.[4] Perhaps, she had delayed marriage so that she could help her widowed mother about the house. Age was not the only difference between them. They had vastly different family backgrounds.

* * *

Edith was born into one of South Australia's old gentry families. She was the granddaughter of Edward Castres Gwynne Snr (1811–1888). The son of an Anglican vicar, Gwynne had arrived in Adelaide in 1838 where he became a noted lawyer, legislator and judge. He also established orchards and vineyards at his 400-acre property, Glynde Place, and farmed at Inman Valley. He became a member of the Adelaide Club in 1880.[5] His son, and Edith's father, Edward Castres Gwynne Jnr (1849–1905), married Mary Mortlock (1853–1944), second daughter of William Ransom Mortlock, in St Peter's Collegiate School chapel on 25 September 1877.

Mortlock had established a well-known South Australian dynasty whose wealth and gentry status were built upon successful milling and pastoral enterprises. He had joined the Adelaide Club in 1869. Edith's father followed her grandfather into the law and was a prominent Adelaide solicitor. Edith's brothers, Charles George Gordon Gwynne, recruited from St Peter's College, and Edward Castres Mortlock Gwynne, both played in the South Australian National Football League for the Norwood Football Club.[6] Edward attended Roseworthy Agricultural College from April 1900 until March 1903, but did not graduate. Charles and Edith did not attend university.[7] Harry Hodgetts' wife had solid links to the Adelaide Establishment, through both her father's and her mother's families.

Little is known of Edith's life at Glynde Place, but almost certainly she enjoyed a lifestyle matching her social standing.

The Adelaide gentry mimicked the customs of their English counterparts. They were related by marriage. They attended balls. The men mingled in the Adelaide Club and rode with the Adelaide Hunt Club while the women paid social calls in the mansions of North Adelaide, East Terrace in the city, Medindie, Walkerville, Kensington, Burnside and Mitcham. Visits to Government House maintained their connections with England. Sons were educated at St Peter's College, with talented scholars proceeding to Trinity College, Cambridge, or Magdalen College, Oxford. Until late in the 19th century girls were often sent to England or France to be 'finished' in a fashionable ladies' school. By the 1890s, however, daughters of the gentry increasingly attended local private-venture schools, which were becoming more academic.[8]

Edith Gwynne attended one of these schools, Miss Martin's School for Girls, which was located first in Miss Martin's Osmond Terrace home in Norwood and then in the city. Results printed in the local press reveal that in the mid-1890s Edith sat, successfully, for freehand art as a pupil of Miss Martin's School, and pianoforte, though it appears she had a private tutor in music.[9] Skills in art and music were part of the 'female accomplishments' that until then had been deemed a suitable education – or training – for the future wives of the gentry.

Miss Martin's School also offered French, German, Italian and Greek as a more academic education better prepared able and privileged young women for university. Miss Martin's former students, Edith Cook and Laura Fowler, had attended the University of Adelaide. Fowler was the first female to graduate in Medicine.[10] Miss Lillie Thompson's School in North Adelaide offered most of the above languages, as well as Grammar, English Literature, Arithmetic, History, Geography, Geology, Botany and Physiology. More than likely, Miss Martin offered a similar

Glynde Place, 1933.
(*Australian Home Beautiful*, Vol. 11, No. 5, 1 May 1933, p. 20.
Courtesy National Library of Australia)

curriculum and aimed at producing well-rounded, 'clever ladies'.[11]

The full complement of the subjects Edith studied, and the extent to which she engaged in social calls, balls and other gentrified activities before her marriage, are unknown. But the home in which she lived speaks volumes about her upbringing. In May 1933, Winnifred Scott of *Australian Home Beautiful* ran a feature article on Glynde Place in which she effused about the garden with its magnificent Moreton Bay fig, under which large Italian jars sat in dappled shade, the old-world charm of the drawing room, its fine old mirror, antique china and silverware, its chest of drawers, handsome desks, jugs and basins. There was a neat staircase, a charming little sitting room and delightful etchings.[12] This was clearly the home of a wealthy, refined and well-educated family, and this was the home in which Edith lived as a small girl and young woman. The house, the people who lived in it and her schooling shaped Edith's values and attitudes. She was an Establishment woman.

* * *

Petersburg Post Office, c. 1907. Petersburg was renamed
Peterborough during World War I.
(Photo: W.J. Angus. Courtesy State Library of South Australia, B 12116)

Harry Hodgetts was born in 1882 in Petersburg (renamed 'Peterborough' in 1917) in the Mid North of South Australia. The family's journey to the area was more convoluted than that of his future wife. Hodgetts' father, Henry Warburton Hodgetts Snr, was born in Toronto, Canada, in 1846. His father died when he was five years old and he then lived with his paternal grandfather, Colonel Thomas Hodgetts. When the Colonel retired from the army several years later, Henry Snr moved with his grandfather to Drogheda in Ireland, and attended the local grammar school.

He moved again with his grandfather, this time to Dublin where he studied medicine. He dropped out after four years and joined the Dublin Post and Telegraph Office as a telegraphist. Aged 35, on 1 August 1881, Hodgetts married Emily Armit Lees and that year the newlyweds sailed for South Australia. Hodgetts arrived bearing a letter of introduction addressed to Sir Charles Todd,

South Australia's Postmaster-General. Todd assigned him to the Petersburg office. In 1887 he was transferred to the Adelaide Post Office. Subsequently he had charge of post offices at Blanchetown, Tea Tree Gully and Burnside. By about 1897, Hodgetts Snr was blind and it was only with his wife's assistance that he carried on until he retired in Toorak Gardens, Adelaide, in 1916.[13]

The former Blanchetown Primary School as it appears today. Hodgetts may have attended the school when his father was Postmaster at Blanchetown Post Office. (Author image)

Harry was the eldest child. Siblings, Richard (1883) and Florence (1886) were also born at Petersburg; Charles (1889) and Ethel (1891) at Norwood when the family lived at 83 Osmond Terrace.[14] Hodgetts Snr was listed in the 1889 South Australian Directory as a civil servant, and while he either owned or rented that property, which has since been demolished, the family was lodged in comfortable, if modest, premises attached to post offices at Petersburg, Blanchetown, Tea Tree Gully and Burnside.[15] Perched on the riverbank and safe from flooding, the Blanchetown office was considered better than average. It was designed originally as a railway station, but the decision to lay a line from Adelaide to Morgan ended that plan.[16] With its central location

St Peter's College, 1938. Although Hodgetts attended for only three terms in 1898, he educated three sons at the school and was an active old scholar. (Courtesy State Library of South Australia, B 10186)

bordering Victoria Square and its magnificent clock tower the Adelaide General Post Office illustrated the importance South Australians placed on correspondence from the 'Old Country' and speedy telegraphic communications. Much smaller in scale and grandeur, rural post offices were nevertheless built of stone, or brick, and added to the solid, permanent feel of South Australian country towns. The same can be said of the country schools that Harry and his siblings would have attended.

Nothing is known of Harry's early schooling, but in 1897, aged 15 years, he attended Old College School, located at 112 Beulah Road, Norwood, and a short distance from the family home. He impressed Principal A.D.R. Leonard, who offered to pay Harry's fees to attend, the following year, either of Adelaide's most prestigious boys' schools: Prince Alfred College or St Peter's

College. Harry chose 'Saints'.[17] He attended the college for only the first three terms of 1898.[18] In October of that year he gained a post-office cadetship. Based in the Accounts Department at the Postmaster General's Department, Adelaide, he was an office clerk until 1910, when he was appointed secretary of The Stock Exchange of Adelaide. He held that position until 1916, when the desire to prosper tempted him to try his hand as a broker. He bought a seat in the Exchange in 1917.[19] By then he had been married for five years and had three children, Edward, Henry (known as 'Gordon') and James. Mary (1918) and Joan (1921) followed shortly after.

* * *

Edith and Harry were from different family backgrounds, but they shared at least one thing in common. As with all non-Indigenous Australians, their forebears were migrants. Edith's grandfather and Harry's father had both migrated to South Australia in search of better prospects. Identifying specific motives is speculative. Both were young and restless. Gwynne quit legal practice in England; Hodgetts Snr, his medical studies. Both had some form of patronage. The first judge of the Supreme Court of South Australia, Sir John Jeffcott, appointed Gwynne clerk of court, despite having no legal right to do so. Who organised Hodgetts' letter of introduction to Todd? Did his high-ranking military grandfather have influence? Both succeeded in their chosen careers, but Gwynne, being the first member of the Bar to be made a Chief Justice, reached far giddier heights.[20] The patriarchs of the Gwynne and Hodgetts families were on the make: they came to South Australia to better themselves. Their family legacies included traits such as ambition, optimism, self-improvement and service to the community.

There were clear differences that may have influenced Harry's subsequent behaviour. Edith's family originated from England and was prominent in the law. Harry's family was from Ireland and, despite some links with the upper ranks of the military, was employed in the postal and telegraphic industries. In South Australia, Edith's family was solidly upper class, Harry's middle at best. Their family status and lifestyles differed markedly. As a self-employed lawyer and son of a former judge, Edith's father had greater power and influence than a telegraphist working in post offices. And, he had attended St Peter's College for more than three terms. Like most women of her time, Edith did not attend university, but her father and one of her brothers, Edward, did. Edward, however, did not graduate. Harry's cadetship provided on-the-job training.

Harry and Edith were married for 37 years. They lived almost all of their married life in the one home where they raised their five children. There is no reason to believe that theirs was not a happy marriage. There is no doubt, however, that Harry Hodgetts married above his class and it begs the question; how much pressure did he feel to provide his wife – and their children – the lifestyle to which she was accustomed? He was largely successful and achieved this until 1945. We shall see ample evidence in his business, sporting, social and charitable activities that he was able, self-assured and generous with his time and money. Former prime minister, Malcolm Turnbull, would have praised him for being 'aspirational'. Yes, he was ambitious, the self-confident man about town, and optimistic. But we shall see that it was unrestrained optimism and self-belief that caused his tragic downfall and, in the end, brought shame upon him and the family name.

Chapter 2

Making Good

As his father's experience had shown, a career in the Post Office offered long-term stability and it does not surprise that Hodgetts entered that service after leaving school. The huge distances between regions and cities in Australia and its isolation from Britain and Europe ensured that colonial governments, and from 1901 the federal government, would monopolise postal and telegraphic services. Private enterprise eschewed the high costs involved.

Postal and telegraphic services were essential to public and private business, military, institutional, family and all other forms of communications. Postal notes facilitated the easy transfer of money, which was especially helpful for poor people. After Federation post offices paid pensions, collected licences and some taxes, and ran branches of the newly created Commonwealth Bank.[1] As a clerk in the Accounts Department of Adelaide's General Post Office, reams of paper passed through Hodgetts' hands. Duties such as filing, adding and subtracting numbers, calculating interest and checking the legality of bank and postal notes honed his numeracy skills and sharpened his eye. But, a hierarchical career path with limited opportunities to rise to the very pinnacle of the Post Office did not appeal, and with his keen eyes on more lucrative, high-profile work Hodgetts resigned in 1910 to take up the position of secretary of the Stock Exchange of Adelaide. When the average adult male wage in South Australia was about £140, Hodgetts' new salary was probably between £250 and £300.[2] This was his first step on the path to wealth.

It is useful here to insert a note of caution. The large amount of information about Hodgetts' business, sporting, charitable and social affairs after 1917 when he bought a seat in the Exchange contrasts markedly with the paucity beforehand. Looking back on his career, it is tempting to conclude that it followed a clearly defined path. This is most unlikely. He seized opportunities and reacted to setbacks as they arose. We shall see that the

A view across King William Street to Adelaide's General Post Office, showing its clock tower, c. 1918. Note the plethora of telegraph wires.
(Courtesy State Library of South Australia, PRG 280/1/21/46)

opportunistic, ambitious and self-confident Hodgetts started with modest aspirations that developed into a strong desire to become a successful, rich and influential man about town. Perhaps his wife's wealthy family background influenced this driven man. Harry Hodgetts carried high expectations.

* * *

Hodgetts was 28 years old when he became secretary of the Exchange. The Exchange was located in a redbrick Federation-style building tucked out of the way in McHenry Street, between Grenfell and Pirie streets and at the rear of buildings fronting King William Street. The call room was on the first floor, where Hodgetts had his office close to the action. Caller H.M. Good – 'the smartest caller of stocks in the colonies' – announced each stock. Brokers indicated whether they were buying or selling and dealing was in lots of a hundred shares. Hodgetts recorded sales and at the end of each trading session read out the record of business. He was the custodian of the Exchange's all-important transaction records, a role that required his undivided attention. Former secretary J.C. Wharton

The former Stock Exchange of Adelaide as it appears today, overshadowed by high-rise buildings.
(Author image)

The call room in 1901. Hodgetts was a familiar figure here between 1910 and 1945.

had been dismissed in 1892 when he was found to be deficient by £486 in his accounts and was unable to repay the outstanding money.[3]

Secretary Hodgetts had many other responsibilities. In 1904, and before his time, the Exchange had floated 72 £200 shares to raise £14,400, and Hodgetts once completed and signed a certificate issued to Thomas Padman, a prominent member of the Exchange between 1895 and 1927.[4] No doubt he signed many others. He corresponded on the Exchange's behalf on all

(Photo: John Gazard. Courtesy State Library of South Australia, B 9066)

sorts of issues. One of his predecessors, for example, had once interviewed the colonial under-treasurer regarding Treasury bills being placed on the Exchange, and another had to advertise the sale of the Exchange's lease on the King William Street premises it had occupied before it moved into the McHenry Street building.[5] Such was the lot of the secretary.

Hodgetts was soon immersed in the culture and practices of the Exchange. As well as being a regular in the call room, he was a familiar figure in the telegraph office, reading room and the impressive vestibule, which were all on the ground floor. The basement housed the Stock Exchange Club, which had a large lounge, billiard room, card room and, of course, a bar.[6] It is likely that he was one of its 320 members. He was secretary and an active member of the Stock Exchange Rifle Club during World War I, topping its rifle class in 1916.[7] A 1915 photograph of the 65 members of the club shows him seated in the front row beside the president, Whitmore Carr. With fists clenched, and resting on his knees in military fashion, Hodgetts appears at ease in the company of Adelaide's leading brokers.[8] From the very beginning of the war the Exchange supported the Lord Mayor's Patriotic Fund and the Belgian Relief Fund, and eventually created its own War Fund. At one stage, Secretary Hodgetts interviewed every Exchange member about making a regular donation to the Belgian Relief Fund.[9]

Hodgetts learned much that would serve him well when he later became a broker – familiarity with 'blue chips', syndicates, speculation, 'sharp practices', 'spectacular successes' and 'spectacular failures'. Knowledge of brokers' jargon was useful. There were 'Coolgardies', 'Brokens', 'good punches', 'The Golden West', the 'Barrier Golconda' and the less admirable 'salting' of mines. He learned that mining could reap great rewards or flop miserably. He learned about industrials, overdrafts, underwriting, futures, scrip, and the old practice of brokers recording clients' orders on their shirt cuffs. There were 'bulls', 'bears' and 'wildcats', bonds, debentures, stocks and, of course, shares. There were 'calls', preference shares and shareholders, order books, profit, loss and more. And he would have done well to note the *Advertiser*'s sound advice that selling on commission for reliable clients was the best way forward for brokers. The *Advertiser* believed that a 'member must be sanguine, yet cautious, speculative yet prudent, quick to seize an opportunity and acute to recognize a danger ...'[10] Wise advice, indeed.

Hodgetts learned about the successful brokers and investors of yesteryear. There were Edward Longson, the 'Prince of Brokers', and George Brookman of Kalgoorlie's 'Golden Mile' fame. Hodgetts rubbed shoulders with more recent brokers of note, including Whitmore Carr, Arthur Walkley, Tony Fotheringham, Theodore Bruce and Charlie Chapple. He learned of the Exchanges' long-established loyalty to the British Empire, exemplified in its support of the Boer War, and of the refined upper-class pretensions of wealthy brokers who lived in mansions in Medindie and North Adelaide. He also knew of the more boisterous brokers who enjoyed a drink or two in hotels within ready reach of the Exchange. The Napoleon, the Gresham and the York were favourites. He learned of the strong link between the Exchange and sport. Two brokers who excelled in sport were Australian cricketer, Clem Hill, who joined the Exchange in 1908, and Jimmie Roberts who played football for the Norwood Club and was a talented runner and tennis player.[11]

* * *

When broker John Brownsword retired in 1916, Hodgetts jumped at the opportunity to buy his seat for £300. As secretary he may have had advanced knowledge of the upcoming vacancy, but whether or not this was true is unknown. Nor is it known how he managed to raise a sum of money that was roughly equivalent to his annual income. Perhaps he had saved the funds; perhaps he borrowed from his or his wife's family.

On his election to the Exchange, Hodgetts entered into a partnership with J.B. Laurie. Their office was located in Cowra Chambers in Grenfell Street, a very short walk from the Exchange.

Cowra Chambers (left) c. 1926. H.W. Hodgetts & Co. was located on the far left of the ground floor, viewed from the street.
(Courtesy State Library of South Australia, B 3312)

Laurie had been a member of the Exchange committee for more than 20 years and a vice-president for three. What better mentor could an aspiring 34-year-old broker want? Five years later Laurie retired and dissolved the partnership. From then on Hodgetts traded as 'H.W. Hodgetts & Co.'. He was on his own and well on his way.[12] Following the British model, brokers had to adhere to strict regulations when advertising. Essentially, they could name their company, advise that they traded in stocks, shares and investments, and give their address and telephone number. Even the font size of their type was controlled. Similar regulations applied to shop-front signage. It was therefore useful to have a prominent profile and location. Cowra Chambers was a short walk from the corner of King William and Grenfell streets, which was the terminus of the trams that serviced the eastern suburbs of Adelaide. At 23 Grenfell Street, Cowra Chambers was strategically placed to catch the attention of cashed-up clients as they alighted from their trams.

Hodgetts had married in October 1912, and the newlyweds had settled into a home in Walsall Street in the developing suburb of Kensington Park. The style of house is unknown but, by 1920, four years into the partnership with Laurie, Hodgetts had moved to 36 Park Road, Kensington Park. This house was a short distance from the Walsall Street home, but more than likely a large step up in price, style and features. This sandstone villa with a lovely garden, clear evidence of successful trading and Hodgetts' growing wealth, exists today. Seven years later, in 1927, a move two doors east to Carlshurst, at 40 Park Road, signalled to the leading citizens of Adelaide that Harry Hodgetts was doing extremely well.[13]

Carl Reinecke, a wealthy accountant and land agent, had built Carlshurst in 1884. It is a two-storey, 13-room sandstone residence with return verandas featuring cast iron posts and detailing. At

Hodgetts' former home at 40 Park Road, Kensington Park, as it appears now. (Photo courtesy Andrea and David Crase)

the time Hodgetts owned the property it was situated on extensive grounds and had stables and a coach-house.[14] In keeping with Exchange brokers' loyalty to all things British, Hodgetts changed the name on the concrete gateposts from Carlshurst to Lichfield. In contrast, Hodgetts' younger brother and fellow stockbroker Charles, lived in his modest, but comfortable, bungalow in Toorak Gardens for 62 years.[15] Within a decade, Hodgetts had become wealthy enough to buy a significant home in Adelaide's eastern suburbs. He owned two motorcars and by 1935 provided Edith an annual allowance of £1400.[16] And, as we shall see, he and his wife entertained generously and in style at Lichfield.

* * *

Carlshurst (Hodgetts called it Lichfield) in the 2020s, viewed from the north-west. (Photo courtesy Andrea and David Crase)

Adelaide's gentry educated their sons at St Peter's or Prince Alfred Colleges and their daughters at one of the leading girls' schools. Attendance at such schools did not guarantee gentry status, but it illustrated the alleged respectability that went hand-in-hand with wealth and the potential for *entrée* into elite society. The Hodgetts children were well served in this regard. All the boys attended St Peter's College; Edward from 1923 to 1932, Gordon from 1924 to 1932, and James from 1926 to 1934.[17] Daughters Mary (1926 to 1935) and Joan (1927 to 1938) attended Girton, literally by walking across the road.[18] It was expensive to educate five children at exclusive private schools. On enrolling their daughters at Girton, parents were required to buy at least five £5 shares – Hodgetts bought 40 – in the company, *Girton Proprietary Limited*. And then there were tuition fees. With the purchase of the minimum number of shares, the first year of a teenage daughter's education at Girton cost about one-fifth of the average male annual income.[19]

Hodgetts had 4000 clients on his office accounts during his business career, demonstrating his reputation as a reliable and successful sharebroker.[20] People from all works of life invested with Hodgetts. Poet, arts patron and barrister Alexander Melrose invested through the entirety of Hodgetts' business career, and Mr and Mrs H.N. Neill were clients for 29 years.[21] Ella Chomley of North Bungaree was just one pastoralist to invest with Hodgetts.[22] There was a former Lord Mayor of Adelaide, a sprinkling of leading lawyers, including Guy Fisher and John Tester, and the Australian cricketer, Arthur Richardson.[23] As the Sydney *Truth* gloated seven years after his downfall, 'were stockbrokers permitted to advertise in less subtle ways, Hodgetts could have hung out the old-time, highly regarded sign "Under Vice-Regal Patronage"'.[24] Indeed, Governor of South Australia from 1939 to 1944, Sir Malcolm Barclay-Harvey, invested with Hodgetts, as did Sir Alexander Hore-Ruthven VC, Governor of South Australia for six years, of New South Wales for one and, as Lord Gowrie, Governor-General of Australia from 1936 to 1944.[25]

So how did Hodgetts go about building his wealth?

* * *

It is impossible to track a detailed course of Hodgetts' trading career. Evidence from his trial showed that he traded in the Broken Hill South and North Broken Hill mining companies. He traded in the Zinc Corporation Ltd, the S.A. Brewing Co., Woolworths, Advertiser Newspapers, Goldsborough Mort & Co., Felt & Textile Ltd., T.J. Richards & Sons, Sands & McDougall and the S.A. Brush Co.[26] He also traded in government loans and bonds. In short, he traded in the usual mining and industrial companies, loans and bonds. By his own admission he began in 1920 with capital somewhere between £2000 and £3000 and relied in difficult times on help from banks, a friend, and other brokers to carry on his business.[27] It was not unusual for brokers to help each other out. We have seen that by 1927 Hodgetts had amassed wealth enough to enjoy a privileged lifestyle at Lichfield. South Australia had enjoyed a run of good seasons, but in that very year, Exchange President, Whitmore Carr, warned brokers to expect a reaction.[28] Broking was a risky business that fluctuated in line with the economy's ever-onward journey, which could be steady or as volatile as a roller coaster.

New York's Wall Street Stock Exchange crashed on 29 October 1929. This started the Great Depression, which affected the world's developed countries by the early 1930s; economies collapsed as markets dried up, and employers who struggled on were forced to retrench workers to cut their losses. In Australia, working-class people and farmers suffered badly, but in South Australia industrial workers were most affected. By 1933 the unemployment rate varied from 13 to 15 per cent in most sectors of the workforce; in the industrial area it was 42.3 per cent. The building industry suffered badly and by 1931 63.3 per cent of its workers were out of work. But the effects of the Depression were not spread evenly and those middle- and upper-class people who retained their incomes were largely unaffected.[29]

When the Depression struck, the Adelaide share market held relatively well compared with the disastrous collapse on Wall Street. Good rains at the end of the year bolstered the hopes of pastoralists who faced heavy falls in the price of their wool. Optimism was short-lived, however. In 1930 the value of Barrier shares – Exchange favourites – plunged. For example, North Broken Hill shares almost halved from £6/5/10 in August 1929 to £3/9/0 in late January 1930. Industrial shares experienced much the same Depression as the miners: Holden's Motor Body Builders' share price collapsed from £1/9/1 in August 1929 to 7/9 in December 1930, and led to a merger with General Motors. Not all companies were severely challenged. The East End Market Company and Brighton Cement, which operated in the depressed building industry, were two that paid dividends, albeit reduced.

With government finances collapsing, NSW Premier Lang urging the repudiation of loans raised in London, and bondholders having to convert their stock into a loan with an interest rate reduced by 22.5 per cent, the loan markets were affected severely. Investors and brokers were nervous. Old hostility to the banks, which were also large bondholders, bubbled once more with accusations that they were manipulating the Depression to their own ends. Brokers dealing in loans were hurting, but by May 1932 the Stock Exchange of Adelaide was doing better than most other companies. This was largely due to gold.[30]

Monday 21 September 1931 brought astonishing news: Britain had dumped the gold standard. Since 1925 the standard had set a guaranteed Bank of England price for gold, but the Depression generated a steady outflow of the precious metal. Banks were running out of gold. The gold standard encouraged deflationary economics as the best response to the Depression, but its lifting allowed more flexible policies that increased demand, promoted recovery and stimulated growth.[31] Initial doubts about the consequences eased in Australia when London's commodities market rose strongly. Adelaide brokers bid Barrier and gold shares higher. When the London Exchange reopened, gold jumped 15/2 to £4/19/7 sterling an ounce, a rise of 18 per cent. Good metal prices stimulated mining and smelting. Brokers did well, especially as the exchange rate was £125 Australian for £100 sterling. Wool prices and shares in Elder Smith & Co. rose solidly. Despite a continued downturn in the prices for lead, zinc, silver, copper and tin, and many other businesses floundering, brokers showed little evidence of financial stress. The recovery was remarkable. In 1931 the average daily turnover in shares rose from 7350 in August to 11,500 in September.[32] Sixteen months later, in December 1932, the average daily turnover of 70,000 shares was 10 times greater. Many sales were in gold stocks, and gold led the brokers' revival.[33] By 1933, the Depression was over for stock and sharebrokers.[34]

In 1934 more than £2 million passed through Hodgetts & Co.'s books.[35] Harry Hodgetts appeared to be prospering, most likely due to burgeoning gold investments. In June 1936, Hodgetts visited the mines of Western Australia with Geoffrey Kyffin Thomas, retired proprietor of the *Register*, a mining engineer and a member of an Adelaide-gentry family. A comprehensive account of Hodgetts' tour was recorded in the *Advertiser*, which did his reputation, and business, no harm. Hodgetts believed that as long as labour and capital cooperated there would be a bright future for gold mining in Western Australia. He and Kyffin Thomas visited many of the de Bernales Group's sites. Hodgetts, was impressed with the thorough and systematic manner in which work was carried out, the efficient managers and the competent staff, with 'no effort being spared to carry out the companies' obligations to their shareholders'. It was an exacting trip over rough tracks on which Hodgetts and Kyffin Thomas encountered camel and mule teams and endured heavy rain, but they managed to inspect mines at Southern Cross, Coolgardie, Kalgoorlie, Menzies, Leonora and Laverton. The pair was greatly encouraged, but Hodgetts reminded investors that it took several years to establish a mine, and that development should proceed slowly.[36]

This was sound advice from a now prominent Adelaide broker. At least one West Australian paper reported that Hodgetts was visiting the state, and by 1936 he had done well enough to feature in *Who's Who: South Australia Centenary, 1936*. Hodgetts' photograph shows a man of confidence, respectability and steadfast determination. The entry mentioned his business activities but focused on his role as a leading official of sporting bodies, his service to the management of educational institutions, and his extensive charity work, all of which we shall explore later.[37] There is no doubt, however, that his sporting and charitable achievements were grounded in his business prowess and success. Without wealth he would have been an unremarkable member of the community.

Hodgetts did not join a syndicate involved in gold exploration and mining in Western Australia. Others had done so with mixed fortune: tales of boom or gloom abounded. Hodgetts knew of, and resisted, the risks. But he did join one syndicate, one that appeared to be based on very sound business practice. In 1940 he teamed with William Lapthorne, Maurice Smith and Arthur Lee to buy Darwin's two hotels. The syndicate planned to modernise the hotels, erect six apartment blocks and build a laundry, ice works and cold stores. Lapthorne told the *Chronicle* that Darwin was developing 'out of all recognition', with a population of over 5000 people.[38] Lee was an experienced hotelier, the owner of the Napoleon and Victoria hotels.[39] The intent was sound and it promised well, but unforeseen danger loomed.

Chapter 3

A Good Sport, An Outstanding Sports Administrator

At the time Hodgetts joined the Stock Exchange of Adelaide, many brokers regularly played sport, with significant success across a range of interests. Several less-active brokers followed the sport of kings. The placing of a bet, the thrill of the race and the resulting sense of joy or despair, at least in a small way, paralleled the action in the call room. The more-active brokers who donned their gloves, picked up a racquet or slipped on their boots could experience similar highs and lows. Sports matches could be as volatile as the market. On the other hand, a good innings on a Saturday might follow on from Friday's 'good punch' with 'Brokens' or 'Coolgardies'.

No broker loved sport more than Hodgetts. Some were better sportsmen, but none matched him as a sports administrator. Financial success as a broker and the support of his staff allowed Hodgetts to engage in the many voluntary administrative duties that made him a household name in Adelaide, and recognised nationally as an important sports administrator.

Hodgetts was more a 'good sport' than an elite sportsman. Most renowned as a cricket administrator, he handled a lacrosse

Above: 'A New Golf Language Introduced By Cricket Legislator' (*Referee*, 30 April 1936, p. 2)

Right: 'Lad of 43' (*Sun*, 27 April 1936, p. 11)

stick with greater proficiency than a cricket bat. As a schoolboy of 14, he took up lacrosse in 1896 when he joined the soon to be defunct East Adelaide Club. He switched clubs and played his first game for the East Torrens B team in 1900.[1] Later, he was promoted to goalkeeper for the A team, a position he held for 12 years. Overall, he played for East Torrens for 20 years and in more than 300 games, including matches played in Queensland, New South Wales and Western Australia.[2] He represented South Australia as goalkeeper against Queensland and Western Australia.[3] Hodgetts was one of the Red and Blues' most loyal players, and it comes as no surprise that he also played cricket for East Torrens. He was 15 when he played his first match in the 1897/1898 season. He played in the East Torrens B team for 24 years, with occasional appearances in the senior side.[4] At age 37, he was selected first drop for the B team when it fronted the West Torrens B team at his old school, St Peter's College, on Saturday 15 February 1919.[5]

Hodgetts enjoyed playing in social matches, even if it was at risk of serious damage to his sporting reputation. At age 43 he turned out to play cricket for the St Peter's Old Boys XI against the School XI. Batting first, the Old Boys made 93, with Hodgetts contributing one run. The School XI made 157 in reply, with Hodgetts returning the bowling figures of 0 for 47, which almost single-handedly accounted for the Old Boys' defeat. It was a scorching hot day, yet 'good sport' Hodgetts pitted himself against men 25 years his junior.[6]

A decade after gracing the Elysian fields of Adelaide's most prestigious boys' school, non-golfer Hodgetts stepped up to tee off on the manicured greens of Sydney's prestigious Manly Golf Club. This happened in a social match that included members of the Australian Board of Control for Cricket and some of the Test players. Present were Board members Aubrey Oxlade, 'Chappie' Dwyer, W.H. Jeanes (secretary), Clem Hill, Roy Middleton and Hodgetts; players included Stan McCabe and Don Bradman. The *Referee* reported that Hodgetts teamed with Bradman and amassed a score of which the latter would have been proud, had the game been cricket. *Referee* focused more on Hodgetts' commentary during the match and ascribed to its light-hearted article the title, 'A New Golf Language Introduced by Cricket Legislator – The Gifted Hodgetts Inspires Envy'. According to *Referee*, Chairman of the Board, Oxlade, was besotted with Hodgetts' linguistic creativity. Acknowledging his lack of proficiency at golf, Roy Middleton chose not to play, but after observing Hodgetts in action, concluded, 'I have a mind to give it a try when I get back to Adelaide. There's someone I know … I could beat.'[7] It is not difficult to imagine the good-natured and congenial banter directed in Hodgetts' direction in the club's striking Georgian-Mediterranean clubhouse after play. Good sport, Hodgetts, could enjoy a joke at his own expense.

Hodgetts was fond of evergreen cricketer Clarrie Grimmett, and fond of playful witticisms at his expense. Grimmett was a champion spin bowler and Hodgetts momentarily stumped him with a 'wrong 'un' on his return from an Ashes tour of England in 1936. As the *Orontes* moored at Outer Harbor on Saturday 25 April, Hodgetts called to Grimmett, 'You know you'll be playing with us (Kensington) this afternoon.' Grimmett's face fell, until he realised that he had been bowled a googly.[8] Two years later in Sydney, Arthur Mailey wrote in the *Sun* that Hodgetts had thought that Grimmett was 63, but was pleased to learn that he was a mere lad of 43. Grimmett was known for his longevity as a cricketer and for his single-minded determination to develop his skill, and Mailey went on to report that in Hodgetts' view the wily spinner had another 20 years cricket ahead of him.[9] Poor Clarrie.

* * *

As early as 1923, when he was 41, the *Observer* said of Hodgetts: 'His generous support of all branches of sport, and his capable administration, has (sic) gained for him an honoured name.'[10] Technically, the *Observer* was over generous in claiming that Hodgetts supported all branches of sport; there is no evidence of him aiding wrestling, boxing and basketball (now known as 'netball'), for example. But Hodgetts' generous support of a number of sports is undeniable and the general tenor of the sentiments the *Observer* expressed was well founded. As we shall see, Hodgetts' 'honoured name' was based largely on his outstanding contributions to the administration of lacrosse and cricket.

Hodgetts, secretary of the Stock Exchange of Adelaide's Rifle Club during World War I, presented his report to the club's Annual General Meeting in February 1916, summarising the year's activities:

> The membership is most satisfactory, and is now 104, of whom 94 are active, and 11 honorary members. The shooting throughout has been highly creditable. Many of the leading shots never previously handled a rifle, and the attendance at the range was, on the whole, excellent.[11]

Hodgetts led by example. He had the second-best attendance at the range and he won the trophy for best shooter over 200 and 300 yards. He attended 45 of the 48 Wednesday evening drill parades.[12] He was at various times president and vice-president of, or held office in, baseball, tennis and football clubs.[13] In July 1925 the *News* reported: 'Headed by that veteran all-round sport, Harry Hodgetts, there is a strong committee working for the improvement of the Kensington Oval.'[14] A year later 3300 people attended a horses-in-action fundraiser at the oval. As President of the Kensington Oval Citizens' Improvement Committee, Hodgetts was on hand to supervise the ring events. In March 1940, he attended the South Australian Hardcourt Tennis Championships at Kadina. At the end of the tournament, he complimented the club on its courts and conduct of the carnival and then the president of the South Australian Lawn Tennis Association gave a brief speech. The president was not named in the report. Hodgetts was.

In 1923 Hodgetts was elected president of the South Australian Olympic Council, a post he held for four years.[15] At the 1923 meeting of the Australian Olympic Federation, he and two other South Australian delegates pressed for the inclusion of the Murray Bridge VIII in the Australian rowing team to compete in the 1924 Paris Summer Olympics.[16] In a fairytale story of 'a crew with no money, no boats and no clubhouse versus wealthy, privileged, city teams', 'The Cods', as they were known, fought off opponents from every state in a qualification race at Port Adelaide to win the right to represent their country.[17] Hodgetts must have been pleased with the outcome.

* * *

It was not uncommon for schoolboys to play club cricket and, as noted above, the 15-year-old Hodgetts donned the pads for the East Torrens Bs in 1897. That he was appointed assistant secretary of the club the following year *was* remarkable.[18] How many 16-year-olds find administrative duties appealing? For most boys, on-field action was their only interest, but not for young Harry. In appointing Hodgetts assistant secretary at such an early age, the East Torrens Cricket Club provided him an opportunity to learn the job and master the requisite skills; recording the minutes of meetings, dealing with correspondence, managing membership, balancing the books, understanding human relationships, and so on.

Similarly, Hodgetts started his career as a lacrosse administrator with the East Torrens Lacrosse Club. He was elected secretary of its Iroquois A team in 1901, and in 1903 was appointed secretary and treasurer of the entire club. He was East Torrens' delegate to the South Australian Lacrosse Association and in 1909 he became its secretary. He went on to hold almost every office in South Australian Lacrosse up to and including those of chairman and president, positions he held for 14 years. He was a selector of South Australian teams, he organised their trips to Victoria, Tasmania and Western Australia, and he organised games against a visiting Canadian team in 1907. In its 1936 summary of Hodgetts, *Who's Who: South Australia Centenary* noted that he had been active in the affairs of the South Australian Lacrosse Association for 30 years. According to 'Right Attack', nobody rendered service to Australian lacrosse greater than Hodgetts.[19]

Several events add colour to Hodgetts' organisational activities. In 1908, he arranged a pre-season trial match between East Torrens and the fledgling Kapunda Lacrosse Club. East Torrens players travelled to Kapunda where they trounced their inexperienced opponents 24 goals to 2. The match was a hit out for East Torrens, but more importantly an opportunity for Kapunda's first-time players to get a taste for lacrosse. The teams mixed socially at half-time, when the afternoon tea tables were decorated in East Torrens' colours of red and blue, and after the match the men gathered at the North Kapunda Hotel for a smoke social.[20]

Hodgetts had a more demanding task when he organised an interstate lacrosse carnival that was held in Adelaide in July 1910. In the *West Australian* 'Lally' argued that this carnival was of even greater value to Australian lacrosse than the Canadian tour three years earlier. And 'Lally' was in no doubt who was responsible for the social success of the carnival:

> The social side of the carnival programme was almost as strenuous as the playing portion. No effort had been spared

to make the stay of the visiting lacrosseurs as enjoyable as possible, and there is no doubt the many merry gatherings at Adelaide will be pleasant topics of conversation amongst Australian lacrosseurs for many years to come. The whole concern passed off without a hitch, which shows how thorough had been the work of Secretary Hodgetts, Assistant-secretary Wilson, and the other members of the South Australian Association.[21]

In March 1915, Hodgetts showed his concern for others. In February, Roy White, of the Holdfast Bay Lacrosse Club and then a member of the Australian Imperial Force, had sent him a letter from Cairo, where Australian troops were training in preparation for active service. White's letter described several lacrosse matches held near the Pyramid of Cheops and named many of the young South Australian players. As a new father Hodgetts sympathised with the parents of these young men who had all volunteered to serve in World War I. He arranged for the letter to be reproduced in the *Mail* of Saturday 27 March so parents could read how their sons were faring.[22] This must have been of some comfort at the time, as news of war's horror was shortly to bode ill. The letter appeared in the *Mail* about one month before Australian and New Zealand troops landed at Gallipoli on 25 April 1915.

* * *

Established in 1897, the East Torrens Cricket Club was an infant when schoolboy Hodgetts was appointed its assistant secretary in 1898. He rose through the ranks to become club chairman, a position he occupied in 1920 when the Kensington District Cricket Club was established. Hodgetts faced a dilemma as he lived in the new club's district, which had been part of East Torrens' zone. The pragmatic Hodgetts maintained a foot in each camp during 1920, and for that year was chairman of both clubs. He remained a friend of East Torrens, but went on to become president of the Kensington Club, the 'Browns'.[23] After just seven years and aged 23 Hodgetts took the next step in his administrative career when, in 1905, he became East Torrens' delegate to the B Grade Association of the South Australian Cricket Association. He served in that capacity for nine years and learned valuable lessons.

Hodgetts rose quickly through the SACA's ranks. He was a member of its ground and finance committee and a trustee of testimonial funds for former South Australian cricketers George Giffen and Jack Lyons. He served on its executive committee, was a member of the Adelaide Oval Building Committee, and once managed an interstate trip for the State team. In 1928 he had served for 10 years as the president of the South Australian Junior Cricket Union, which controlled over 3000 young players. By 1936, Hodgetts had been involved in the organisation of South Australian cricket for over 35 years.[24]

In 1923, Hodgetts first represented South Australia on the Australian Board of Control for International Cricket and became one of the state's three delegates from 1926. He remained a delegate from 1926 until 1945 when he resigned.[25] The Board discussed in its meetings anything and everything that related to cricket – arrangements for home and international tours, players' allowances, the Test-team captaincy whenever a new skipper was needed, the rules of the game, umpires, matters relating to the Sheffield Shield competition, and the election of a new Board Chairman every three years, among other issues. In the 1930s, for example, a new leg-before-wicket law was introduced in grade

William Charles Brooker took this c. 1928 photograph of Adelaide Oval, which Hodgetts visited frequently.
(Courtesy State Library of South Australia, PRG 1316/4/266)

cricket and in 1936 the Board of Control planned to trial it in the Sheffield Shield competition. Designed to stop defensive 'pad play', under the new law a batsman could be given out LBW to a ball that pitched outside off stump. The Board asked the Marylebone Cricket Club to adopt the law in time for England's forthcoming 1936/1937 Australian tour. The MCC did change the law, but it came into effect in 1937 after the Fifth Test, which finished on 3 March.[26] Delegates had specific duties at various times. In 1931, Hodgetts was one of three members of a sub-committee formed to choose umpires for future Test matches.[27]

The Board had to deal with difficult matters, none more so than 'bodyline'. To combat Bradman's dominance in its 1932/1933 Australian Ashes tour, England's captain, Douglas Jardine, devised a plan of attack in which his strike bowler, Harold Larwood, targeted the batsman's body and the leg side was crowded with fielders. There was, then, no limit on the number of fielders a captain could place behind square leg. These belligerent tactics were dangerous. The Australian Board of Control had considered lodging a protest, but was uncertain about how to proceed and divided over taking any action at all. Simmering tensions turned hostile when Larwood struck Australian Captain Bill Woodfull near his heart in the Adelaide Test on 14 January 1933. The crowd hurled abuse at the English players, Larwood and Jardine in particular, and matters threatened to get out of hand. Four members of the Australian Board of Control were present, William Kelly from Victoria, and the three South Australian delegates, Bernard Scrymgour, Roy Middleton and Hodgetts. Witnessing the incident firsthand, they drafted a telegram of protest and sent it to the Chairman, Dr Allen Robertson, who forwarded it to the other Board members for their response. Board opinion was divided, NSW and Queensland delegates were opposed, possibly in fear of losing their upcoming Tests, the telegram was said to be 'clumsy, inelegant and ill-formed' and Bill Woodfull and Don Bradman refused to add their names to it.[28] In the event, a telegram was sent lodging a protest that Hodgetts had helped draft:

AUSTRALIAN BOARD OF CONTROL TO MCC, January 18, 1933:

Bodyline bowling assumed such proportions as to menace best interests of game, making protection of body by batsman the main consideration. Causing intensely bitter feeling between players as well as injury. In our opinion is unsportsmanlike. Unless stopped at once likely to upset friendly relations existing between Australia and England.[29]

Hodgetts was heavily involved in the Board's deliberations and control of cricket. That he served for 19 years underlines the value of his contribution. He was highly regarded and in 1939 the Brisbane *Telegraph* suggested that as it was South Australia's turn at the helm Hodgetts was likely to be elected the new chairman of the Board.[30] That did not happen. At this time New South Wales and Victoria monopolised the chairmanship, with Oxlade (NSW) and Robertson (Vic.) sharing it intermittently for three-year stints from 1927 to 1952, except when World War II intervened.[31] Hodgetts might have lost out to the two most powerful states, but his work at the highest level gave him insights into the machinations of Australian cricket, which he soon used to his and South Australia's advantage.

Telegraph, Brisbane.
(19 August 1939, p. 7)

In September 1928, the *News* featured an article summarising Hodgetts' sporting and sports administration careers in its page devoted to the opening of the new cricket season: 'Mr. H.W. Hodgetts'.
(*News*, 27 September 1928, p. 15)

Chapter 4

Brokering a Deal with Bradman

In 1934 Hodgetts brokered a deal that saw the 26-year-old cricketer, Don Bradman, transfer from New South Wales to South Australia. Bradman agreed to reside in Adelaide for six years, play cricket for local club Kensington, and for South Australia and Australia when required. In return, he worked as a stockbroker's clerk in H.W. Hodgetts & Co., with time off to play cricket. Bradman's annual salary was £700, reduced to £500 when he toured abroad with the Australian team.[1] In a separate agreement, Bradman signed a new three-year contract with his former Sydney employer, the menswear store, F.J. Palmer & Son, to act as its Adelaide sports-goods representative.[2]

By 1934 the cricket world rated Bradman a champion batsman. The *Sydney Morning Herald* pointed out that Bradman held many records, and that he had made 118 runs for New South Wales in his very first match, played against South Australia at Adelaide Oval in December 1927. In 1930 he amassed 334 against England in Leeds and in 1932, 299 not out against South Africa in Adelaide. On the interstate front his huge scores stood out: 340 not out against Victoria, and 452 not out against Queensland.[3] New South

Wales had a prolific run scorer, a master batsman who could almost single-handedly win it the Sheffield Shield. So why, then, did Bradman make the shift? How did this happen? Who stood to gain, who would lose? How was Bradman's move received? How important was Hodgetts' role?

* * *

Bradman was not the only, or the first, cricketer to cross the border to play for South Australia. Sign-writer and spin bowler Clarrie Grimmett had transferred from Victoria in 1924 when businessmen Joe Travers – a State selector – and Eddie McCarron arranged work for him in Adelaide. Grimmett played for local club Kensington, South Australia and Australia, taking 1424 first-class wickets at 22 runs apiece.[4] The South Australian Cricket Association was delighted to have a world-class leg spinner and about a decade later, to bolster its batting, set its sights on Tasmanian's Jack Badcock, who was also being pursued by Victoria. Businessmen again played their part. Adelaide furniture manufacturer J.L. Brown offered Badcock employment as a sales representative, and the SACA completed negotiations. Who better to do the deal than a member of its executive committee, Henry Warburton Hodgetts Jnr?

Hodgetts won from Badcock a promise that if he ever transferred to the mainland, South Australia would have first call on his services.[5] Badcock transferred in 1934. The SACA had established a successful recruitment model in the age of amateur cricket: the use of prominent businessmen working at arm's distance to entice established cricketers with offers of guaranteed employment. This could only benefit South Australian cricket. Badcock transferred in the same year as Bradman, the *Chronicle* declaring, 'The presence of the world's best batsman and one of the most promising colts in Australian cricket will make South Australia a powerful factor in the Sheffield Shield competition.'[6] Monash University academics Tom Heenan and David Dunstan noted that with Bradman, Badcock and Grimmett in the side the gate takings at Adelaide Oval would boost the SACA's coffer.[7]

If enticing Bradman to Adelaide were a victory for the SACA, would it also benefit its proxy negotiator, Harry Hodgetts? Yes. According to Roland Perry, 'Hodgetts was as shrewd as his pin-striped suit inferred', his prosperous appearance clearly indicating to potential clients that he was doing very well, and that they might too with his guiding hand on their investments.[8] In negotiating the deal with Bradman both Hodgetts and the SACA stood to gain. By 1934, Hodgetts had cultivated a friendship with Bradman, who stayed at his Kensington Park house whenever New South Wales played in Adelaide. Hodgetts had first-hand knowledge of Bradman's character and potential business skills. He discovered that Bradman was taciturn and not fond of publicity but had a gift for arithmetic calculation, planning and strategy. He was clean cut and his integrity was evident to all cricket fans.[9] These traits suited well a career in stockbroking, though there was no evidence of the flair that his future boss exhibited. Bradman would make a very handy broker's clerk, who might eventually develop into a broker.

None of this was lost on Hodgetts. In press interviews at the announcement that Bradman was moving to Adelaide, Hodgetts stressed that he was 'very fond of Don' and that he was looking forward to having him in his firm. He added that Bradman was good with figures and had worked in offices for five years. With an eye to a mutually satisfactory future, Hodgetts declared: 'When he (Bradman) had absorbed the atmosphere of the business, there is no doubt that he will be an asset to the Stock Exchange.'[10]

Stockbrokers were subject to strict regulations when they advertised for business, so Hodgetts was more than happy to have the most famous name in sport associated with his business. From the beginning, Hodgetts had Bradman greet and meet clients and see their wishes were carried out.[11] Hodgetts used his own public sports identity to promote his business. Much could be achieved mixing with clients and potential clients. He mentored Bradman in this. Despite Hodgetts' membership of the Adelaide Club, the thought that Bradman, a carpenter's son and cricketer from rural New South Wales, might be accepted was beyond the pale. So, Bradman joined the genteel Mount Osmond Golf Club with its idyllic hills setting above Adelaide, and complied with Hodgetts' advice: 'Never let a potential client lose badly.' To enhance his protege's reputation even more, Hodgetts lobbied the SACA to appoint Bradman captain of South Australia, and to make him a State selector.[12] The deal broker intended to profit from the deal.

Bradman knew that he lived in an age when it was impossible to make a living from sport alone. He was mindful that players needed at least part-time work aside from their sport and he believed that they should have a trade or profession that would support them when their playing days were over. He also believed that they were better people for it, and that work made them more grounded in the real world.[13] The story of growing up in Bowral, the stump, golf ball and rainwater tank stand are the stuff of legend and do not warrant attention here.

Bradman left Bowral High School in 1922 after completing his Intermediate examination. At first, he worked in Percy Westbrook's local real estate business, before moving in 1928 to the Sydney branch. At that time, he broke into first-class cricket and very soon the runs flowed and business deals followed. He allowed William Sykes Ltd to use his name on their bats, he agreed to work for Mick Simmons Ltd, sporting goods distributors, and, in 1931, he accepted a packaged contract with Associated Newspapers, radio station 2UE and Sydney menswear retailer, F.J. Palmer. These contracts were doubly important to Bradman as they were struck during the Great Depression, and in April 1932 he married Jessie Menzies.[14] All the contracts allowed him to continue playing cricket.

Some of Bradman's contracted work did not sit well with the Australian Board of Control. In 1930, Bradman spent his free time writing a book about the current Ashes tour of England. The book was serialised in the *Star*, a London evening newspaper. This was a breach of his tour contract and the Board fined him £50.[15] In 1931, the professional cricketer playing for the Accrington Cricket Club in the Lancashire League withdrew at the last minute. Another was found, but the club finished 12th. In desperate straits, it 'offered terms to the number one batsman in the world, Don Bradman'. The offer was reputed to be worth £500 a season for a three-year contract. After weeks of speculation and the club increasing the sum to £600, Bradman telegrammed his rejection: 'Regret decline offer. Appreciate pleasant nature of negotiations. Writing full details, Bradman.' If Bradman had accepted the offer, he would have breached the terms of his contract with the Board, which prevented him from playing for an English club before 1932.[16] Disputation with the Board was not a good look for Bradman.

In February 1934, the *Australian Worker* noted that every season there was talk of Bradman leaving New South Wales to live and play elsewhere. As well as the attempt to lure him to the Lancashire League, rumours abounded that Bradman had been offered a good job in Melbourne.[17] Bradman was considering his future, a situation not lost on Hodgetts. Bradman's journalism was precise, astute and well structured, but it lacked the flair that some tabloids favoured. Radio was never going to be his forte. Sensationalism was not the Bradman style. Neither was signing autographs in Palmer's sports goods department.[18] But the Hodgetts deal fitted the bill for Bradman. It offered security, the chance to learn broking and to become a broker. It provided what he craved most of all, a career away from cricket. And it was about numbers, analysis and quick decision-making, playing to his strengths. Bradman put it this way:

> Throughout the past few years, I have lived cricket. I have been connected with sports goods, journalism, where I had to write cricket, and broadcasting where I had to talk cricket from morning to evening. I had no chance of getting away from the game. It had become not a sport but my life. Now, with business interests not concerned with the game I can devote my spare time to cricket and when I am away from the field I need not worry unduly about the game.[19]

Heenan and Dunstan presented a more critical view of Bradman. They asserted a number of things. Bradman had an obsessional self-regard that made him unpopular with many cricketers, including some of his teammates. On the field, English captain, Norman Yardley, considered him tough, unrelenting and not above gamesmanship. Bradman was also more comfortable with adults who indulged him, and he saw the 52-year-old Hodgetts as a reassuring and powerful older person whom he might use to his advantage. Bradman realised that cricket would allow him to become rich and climb the social ladder. He loved numbers and learned early that big scores at the crease could leverage lucrative sporting and business deals. Heenan and

Brokering a Deal with Bradman

Dunstan also noted his less-than harmonious relationship with the Australian Board of Control and that when it questioned his off-field business activities he threatened to join the Lancashire League. The Board, mindful of Bradman's drawing power at the gate, did not wish to lose its major drawcard. Thus, Hodgetts, a Board member, SACA powerbroker and leading stockbroker, offered Bradman a deal. Heenan and Dunstan rejected the theory that consequently Bradman was no longer financially dependent on cricket, that he was now a part-time stockbroker's clerk and an amateur cricketer in his spare time. They cited historian Chris Harte who revealed in his 1993 *A History of Australian Cricket* that the SACA paid £500 of Bradman's annual income, with Hodgetts paying the remaining £200. In Heenan and Dunstan's view, Bradman espoused the values of the amateur sportsman, but behind the scenes he was self-serving and pecuniary. In their view:

'Don Is Now Our Don'
(*News*, 13 March 1934, p. 1)

Don Is Now Our Don

Don Bradman reached Adelaide to-day, a day ahead of the announced date of his arrival, and now is a South Australian if only from a residence view point.

Bradman left the express at Mount Lofty, and completed his journey to the home of Mr. H. W. Hodgetts at Kensington Park by motor car.

Both Mr. and Mrs. Bradman are pleased to be in Adelaide, and are looking forward to their life here. Don said that it was no secret that he had been seeking for a long time a career entirely apart from cricket.

"For years now I have been playing cricket, talking cricket, writing cricket, and living cricket," he said. "I do not think that is good for anybody. I think I have achieved my ambition by taking a position here."

While he has never been associated with stock and share work before, Bradman thinks his seven years in a real estate business will stand him in good stead. He will complete some business arrangements with Mr. Hodgetts this week. Arrangements for his future

DON BRADMAN is welcomed to Adelaide.

home will be left until he returns from England.

It was thought that Bradman would practise with the Kensington Club this week, but he said he had no intention of taking a bat in his hands until the team reached Perth. He will join the side here next Tuesday.

Mrs. Bradman will stay in Adelaide until after her husband leaves for England. She will then go to live with her parents in New South Wales until a short time before Don returns to Australia.

According to myth, Bradman joined Hodgetts to learn the stockbroking game. In reality, Bradman's job was cricket. Most of his wage was not paid by Hodgetts, but by the South Australian Cricket Association (SACA). Bradman was a part-time stockbroker's clerk and fulltime professional cricketer. In a world that still celebrated sport for the love of it Bradman was a 'shamateur'.[20]

Heenan and Dunstan argued that Bradman leveraged the deal with Hodgetts and the SACA.[21] This may be true, but Bradman was not the instigator and sole beneficiary. It was Hodgetts who approached Bradman, and all signatories stood to benefit from the deal.

* * *

On Monday 19 February 1934, Bradman advised the New South Wales Cricket Association that he would be moving to Adelaide. The Association recorded its appreciation of what Bradman had done for New South Wales cricket and wished him well for the future.[22] Bradman and Jessie travelled by train to Adelaide under the name of 'Lindsae', arriving on Tuesday 13 March. The Railways authorities made special arrangements for the *incognito* celebrities, and stopped the train at Mount Lofty in the Adelaide Hills so they did not have to disembark at the Adelaide Railway Station. Hodgetts met and drove them to his home where they stayed for a week prior to Bradman joining the Australian team in Tasmania for a practice match in preparation for its upcoming tour of England. Meanwhile, the Kensington District Cricket Club committee hastily convened and elected Bradman a member. This, and by residing with Hodgetts for a week, made him eligible to play for South Australia when he returned from the Ashes tour. During this week Bradman and his wife made arrangements to live in Kensington Park.²³ As well as the major city newspapers, rural and regional papers such as the *Scone Advocate,* Launceston's *Examiner,* the *Manning River Times and Advocate for the Northern Coast Districts of New South Wales,* and Western Australia's *Avon Argus and Cunderdin-Meckering-Tammin Mail* reported the move.²⁴ Bradman's move was big news and its reporting sold papers.

Jessie Bradman. (*South Australian Homes & Gardens,* 2 July 1934, p. 55)

The press coverage of Bradman's move was expansive and overwhelmingly positive, even in New South Wales. The general view was that it would be good for Bradman, and there was relief he would not be lost to Australian cricket. In South Australia the *Advertiser* reported that the news was most satisfying to cricket and business circles. It thought that Bradman's presence would improve the standard of batting at both State and club levels. It voiced the views of cricket identities. Local Test selector, Dr C.E. Dolling, thought that while it would benefit South Australian cricket, even more importantly, Bradman would still be available to play for Australia. Victor Richardson, Clem Hill and Joe Travers – by then a State selector – all agreed. They were delighted by the news and Hill thought it the best thing ever to have happened to South Australian cricket. In excited anticipation, Travers already had one hand on the Sheffield Shield. James Gosse, the managing director of George Wills & Co., believed that Bradman had rightly looked to the future and realised the game was just that, a game.[25] New South Wales Board of Control member, Frank Cush, was sorry to see Bradman leave, but was pleased the move was good for his health and for South Australia and that he was not lost to the Test team.[26]

'Old-timer's' letter sent to the *Sun* implied that some New South Wales cricket fans were not entirely pleased with Bradman, and he urged the State's young cricketers to step up to the mark:

> TO YOUNG CRICKETERS
>
> 'Old-timer' loves cricket: –
> Are we downhearted? No! New South
> Wales has always produced first-class
> cricketers – and always will. No matter
> with what State Don Bradman plays, he
> will always belong to us, and when he
> returns to hit sixers in our Cricket Ground
> against us we will give him a royal
> welcome. It just behoves our young
> cricketers to set to work to fill the gap and
> keep our end up.[27]

* * *

Hodgetts played a key role in winning Bradman for South Australia. He had cultivated their friendship early in Bradman's career. It is unimaginable that they had not discussed Bradman's business future when he stayed at Lichfield whenever interstate cricket brought him to Adelaide. If Heenan and Dunstan are correct, Hodgetts was the powerful older person Bradman sought out, for his own advantage. Hodgetts was powerful, as we have

Don and Jessie Bradman with their Chevrolet Master
in front of Lichfield in 1935.
(Courtesy *South Australian Home & Gardens*, 1 March 1935, p. 46)

seen. Hodgetts acted on behalf of and for the South Australian Cricket Association and a Board of Control that did not want its star batsman playing for another country, and the wily Hodgetts knew the advantage to be gained from having Don Bradman on his staff. Hodgetts was more than the middleman between the SACA and Bradman. If Bradman and the SACA benefited from the deal, so did Hodgetts. It was the SACA that paid Bradman's reduced income when he was away playing cricket, not Hodgetts.

Chapter 5

Service Without Reward

The Adelaide gentry practised the *noblese oblige* that their English counterparts followed. By the 19th century, the English gentry had come to believe that wealth carried a responsibility to serve the common good, to do noble deeds. A growing number of enlightened manor lords cared in a material sense for their tenants, while others, including some wealthy industrialists and merchants, were generous benefactors to a range of community services.

In South Australia, philanthropists Sir Walter Hughes, Sir Thomas Elder, Robert Barr Smith, Peter Waite and Sir Langdon Bonython gave generously to the University of Adelaide. So too did Edith Hodgetts' first cousin, John Andrew Tennant Mortlock, who played the role of country gentleman at the family estate – Martindale Hall in the Clare Valley. In 1926 he donated £2000 to the Waite Institute Campus of the University of Adelaide, and in 1936 £25,000 for research into soil and pasture management. In death he bequeathed £73,000 to cultural organisations and charities. The Mortlock Wing of The State Library of South Australia is named in his honour.[1]

Doubtless, leading-citizen Hodgetts was aware of Mortlock's generosity and the broader notion of serving the community. However, he did not possess huge disposable wealth, and looked for other ways to serve. English public schools such as Eton, Rugby and Winchester influenced the values advocated in the Australian educational systems and institutions, including independent, fee-paying schools. These included corporate spirit, loyalty, fellowship, sportsmanship and service. As the first Chairman of the Board of the Girton Proprietary School for Girls, Hodgetts supported its advocacy of service without reward. Doing good deeds and giving selfless leadership sat well with the school's clientele, and Harry Hodgetts.[2] Other organisations, such as the international Christian movement Toc H, espoused similar views that flowed on to the general public. Hodgetts duly set out to serve his community.

Hodgetts gave outstanding service as a sports administrator, but his community service reached far wider and deeper than the breadth and depth of lacrosse and cricket fields. He served educational and service institutions for long periods and readily volunteered for short-term fundraising activities. He applied his managerial and accounting skills to good effect. His wife and children also served. He willingly donated money to worthy causes.

* * *

Hodgetts valued education. He did not attend university, and little is known of his children's post-school education and qualifications. When they finished their secondary schooling, Henry (Gordon), Mary and Joan were 17 years old, Edward 19 and James 20. They all attended fee-paying schools and this speaks of the value Hodgetts placed on education – and his social aspirations. Like his mother before him, Edward studied music privately and in May 1933 he played a piano piece during a public concert; in that same year Mary topped the State Leaving Physiology examination.[3] Only Edward and Mary went on to study at the University of Adelaide. In 1935 Edward was living at St Mark's College, a residential college affiliated with the university, and studied law subjects as a non-graduate student. About the same time, Mary took two subjects as a Bachelor of Science student. Like their paternal grandfather before them, neither graduated.[4]

Adelaide's St Peter's College is nestled among streets whose names resonate with the public schools and great universities of England. Named after public schools, there are Eton Lane, Harrow Road and Marlborough Street. Oxford, Baliol, Pembroke and Trinity streets are linked to Oxford University. Magdalen Street is the one named for its link to Cambridge University. The Rev. Kenneth Julian Faithfull Bickersteth was appointed headmaster of St Peter's in 1919. Bickersteth was educated at Rugby and Christ Church, a constituent college of Oxford University. It comes as little surprise that Bickersteth moved a motion in 1920 at the Anglican Synod of the Diocese of Adelaide that a committee be appointed to explore steps to establish a residential college for students of the University of Adelaide. Following a public meeting in the Adelaide Town Hall on 29 May 1922, Executive and General Committees were elected to oversee the founding of the college. An appeal was launched and in 1923 an agreement was reached to purchase the Downer Family residence on Pennington Terrace, near St Peter's Cathedral in North Adelaide. The college was named after St Mark, to honour the name of the saint on whose day the ANZAC landing at Gallipoli occurred. Archibald Grenfell Price was appointed its first Master.[5]

St Mark's staff and students, 1935. Hodgetts is fifth from the left in the front row. Master Archibald Grenfell Price is on his left. (Courtesy St Mark's College, 1935, St Mark's College record. Special supplement, the history of the college and college register 1925–1935, National Library of Australia, p. 27, Nla.obj2334401335)

St Peter's College old boy Harry Hodgetts was a member of the Executive Committee and a leading founder of St Mark's. Hodgetts focused on financial matters and he played a key role in securing the late Sir John Downer's property. He loaned the money needed to secure options to purchase the property and adjoining land owned by wholesale grocers David and James Fowler. These properties were valued at about £10,000. When, on 16 March 1923, the Finance Committee was authorised to make the purchase, the only money it had at its disposal was that which Hodgetts had loaned. Several times in the following months he loaned more money; on one occasion the amount was almost £3000. As soon as the options to purchase the properties were accepted the Executive Committee published a prospectus and launched an appeal to raise £30,000. Not surprisingly, Hodgetts was a member of the group that canvassed for funds. By May the committee had received enough cash and promises to proceed with the purchases.⁶ Hodgetts committed to St Mark's founding generously in time and money and an appreciative Executive Committee saw that he was repaid. In 1930, he was elected to the college's Finance Committee and, interestingly, to the Education Committee.⁷ That the college valued him greatly was underlined when he sat in the front row to the right of Master Grenfell Price in the 1935 photograph of its governors, staff and students.⁸

* * *

Hodgetts was the Chairman of the Board of Directors of Girton virtually from its establishment in 1926 until 1945. As chairman he was closely involved in the management of the school, overseeing its financial position and general educational policies and practices and helping to resolve occasional disputes between headmistresses, staff and parents. As he lived across the road from the school, he was more concerned with the day-to-day business of the school than is normally the case for a chairman of directors. Men dominated the Board, but the four headmistresses Hodgetts worked with were 'new women', all more highly educated than he. The first two, Dorothy Angove and Edith Bishop, had both graduated Bachelor of Arts, while the third, Dorothea Poole, was a Master of Arts and holder of Cambridge University's Medieval and Modern Languages Tripos. Dorothy Yates, the fourth headmistress, graduated Bachelor of Science and held Cambridge University's Teachers' Training Certificate.⁹ While some women had made substantial gains in the first decades of the 20th century, female teachers then had to resign on marriage. All of these headmistresses were single, except for Mrs Angove who was a widow raising two sons. That men, led by a person without tertiary qualifications, dominated

A share certificate for Girton Proprietary Limited showing
Director H.W. Hodgetts Jnr's signature.
(John Davis, *Principles and Pragmatism*, Volume 1, p. 40)

the Board of a school for girls illustrates the patriarchal nature of the era. Hodgetts was comfortable with this situation, and took to his work with unquestioned authority, determination and energy.

Lillie Smith – wife of stockbroker James Smith – had operated Girton House Girls' Grammar School at Kent Town from 1915 to 1925 when ill health forced her to sell. When the Church of England refused to buy the school, Mrs W.H. Irwin established a provisional committee in order to reconstitute it as a parents' proprietary school – the Girton Proprietary School for Girls.[10] Hodgetts and fellow stockbroker Gordon Sunter were members of the Provisional Committee that drew up the prospectus of Girton Proprietary Limited. Its registered office was located in Cowra Chambers – home to H.W. Hodgetts & Co. – from which 5000 £5 shares were sold to raise capital of £25,000, and prospective parents were obliged to buy at least five shares on enrolling their daughters. It is not likely that Hodgetts charged commission, given that he was one of the four people who each bought 40 shares. As well as making a significant financial contribution to establish the new school, Hodgetts took over as chairman of the all-male Board of Directors after interstate business commitments prevented its initial Chairman, W.J. Masson, from carrying out his duties.[11]

When the Kent Town property proved inadequate, the Board purchased for £5800 Mark Ridgway's property in Holden Street, Kensington Park, even though it failed to impress Headmistress Angove. Chairman of the Board Hodgetts was the lead signatory on the contract of sale for the property. Classrooms were built and the school moved in at the beginning of the 1927 school year. To cover expenses, the Board made calls of £1 each on the 690 shares held in June 1926 and issued another 500 shares. Hodgetts was one of five who each guaranteed £500 to cover a bank overdraft of £2500.[12] Transferring the school from Kent Town to Kensington Park was a bold move by a courageous Board led by a generous and competent businessman with strong finance skills.

In his two decades as Chairman of the Board, Hodgetts led Girton through the Great Depression and World War II. In an era without government funding for independent schools these were challenging years. Despite its well-heeled clientele, Girton struggled financially. It provided scholarships and bursaries to girls from within and without the school.[13] When some parents struggled to pay fees the Board allowed extensions, and in one case, to keep two sisters at the school, it accepted the family piano in lieu of fees, at a loss of £13.[14] Hodgetts' Board had a kind heart.

Girton was a non-denominational school, but *de facto* Anglican in practice. It had a close relationship with the Church of England, as did its directors, including Hodgetts. In 1932 the Diocesan

Hodgetts (left) and Archibald Grenfell Price with teacher Miss T. Hardy at Girton's first inter-house sports day, 26 July 1929.

(Photo courtesy Pembroke School Archives)

Board of Education asked Girton to consider becoming a Church of England school. Church backing, however, would come at a cost, the teaching of the Anglican creed. Hodgetts and three other directors examined and rejected the offer, possibly fearing that it would lessen the school's appeal to non-Anglican families at a time when it was trying to boost enrolments.[15] In 1937 extensions were made to the boarding house to accommodate an increased number of girls. It cost £559 and to speed things along Hodgetts lent £500. But the school's bank overdraft concerned the Board, which called on parents and supporters to act as guarantors. Hodgetts was one of three men who each guaranteed £500. But, just two years later, it was the bank that was concerned about the school's £3000 overdraft. The school made losses in 1939 and 1940, by which time the situation was grave enough for the Board to authorise Hodgetts to ask the Church of England to take over the school. The Church declined, and the school struggled on.[16]

Hodgetts was a hands-on chairman. He presided over the annual speech nights; he acted as a steward or judge at the inter-house sports days, and he attended fundraising events. Mrs Hodgetts played her part too and they were both present to receive Lady Zara Hore-Ruthven, wife of the Governor,

Entrance to Girton, Kensington Park.
(Photo courtesy Pembroke School Archives)

when she attended an American Tea organised by the Girton Mothers' Association in April 1934.[17] When some senior girls played informal cricket matches on Kensington Oval in 1935, Hodgetts donated the money to purchase the equipment and arranged for Bradman to help the girls choose bats, no doubt ones manufactured by Sykes & Sons.[18] The Board oversaw the financial management of the school and left matters of staffing, curriculum and student discipline to the headmistress. There were two occasions, however, when under Hodgetts' leadership the Board intervened in curriculum and staffing matters.

In 1931, during the Depression, Headmistress Angove reduced expenditure. As there were few girls taking Arithmetic and Physiology in the Intermediate-Examination curriculum, Angove discontinued the two subjects, saving £50. Some parents complained directly to Hodgetts who called a special meeting of the Board. He believed it should have had some input into the decision not to include Arithmetic. At that meeting Angove explained the reasons for her decision and reminded the Board that the terms of her contract gave her sole responsibility for the curriculum. At its next meeting the Board resolved to restore Arithmetic to the curriculum, as long as at least seven girls opted to take the subject, and that the cost did not exceed £21. Angove believed strongly in her autonomy and tendered her resignation. Mrs W.H. Irwin and Gordon Sunter interviewed her on the Board's behalf and convinced her to withdraw her resignation. A compromise was reached. The Board would not interfere with the headmistress in curriculum and management matters unless a resolution to do so was passed at a Board meeting, and Angove agreed to confer with the Board whenever she proposed a major adjustment. Hodgetts and the Board were relieved and expressed their hope that future relations would be more cordial.[19] Angove was a determined woman and she resented Hodgetts and the Board interfering in her domain. But Girton was then a parents' proprietary school and maybe Hodgetts believed the Board had a responsibility to act on behalf of shareholder, fee-paying parents.

In 1933 peripatetic part-time music teacher John Dempster

thrice refused Headmistress Bishop's request to practise a particular hymn on the grounds that he was in charge of the class and that he would not tolerate interference. Hodgetts became aware of the incident and called a special meeting of the Board at which Bishop confirmed what had happened. This time, the Board intervened on the headmistress's behalf and consequently Dempster apologised to Bishop. In August 1934, Bishop advised Dempster that his contract would be terminated at the end of the year. Dempster resigned at the end of Term Two, complained to the Board about the manner in which Bishop had treated him, and threatened legal action to claim lost income. The school's lawyers denied responsibility and no more was heard. Hodgetts' voluntary work may have been rewarding, but its path was not always straightforward.

Late in 1931, Headmistress Angove received an invitation from the Citizens' League to attend a meeting of old scholars of independent schools 'with the object of having the duties of Citizens brought before the Scholars during the last fortnight of the school year'. Angove sought the Board's advice, which was that 'the objects of the meeting being non-political, the headmistress was at liberty to attend'. There is no evidence that Angove attended, but the issue sheds light indirectly on Hodgetts' political views and allegiance.

The Citizens' League was a conservative organisation that promoted itself as 'non-party' and 'non-political', but it was anti-Labor and actively campaigned against the Scullin Government in 1931. It advocated loyalty to God, King and country and equality of sacrifice during the Depression. Historian Michael Cathcart labelled its leader, Captain E.D.A. Bagot, 'a pugnacious, self-proclaimed fascist' who wanted Sir John Monash to be made 'controller or dictator' of Australia. By September 1931 the

Citizens' League claimed to have a membership of 20,000. But Master of St Mark's College, Archibald Grenfell Price, mustered all the anti-Labor forces into an 'Emergency Committee', thereby holding Bagot's extremism in check. Hodgetts and the Girton Board's claim that the Citizens' League was non-political does not stand scrutiny. Hodgetts knew Grenfell Price well through St Mark's College. It is inconceivable that Hodgetts was unaware of the nature and aims of the Citizens' League, and the more moderate Emergency Committee. And, the Citizens' League invitation was made to Angove during the federal election campaign that saw the defeat of James Scullin's Labor Government.[20] Bagot had identified Girton as a school that espoused values such as loyalty and duty; values that upheld the prevailing social structure, values that its conservative clientele supported.

Fellow stockbroker Andrew Young spoke at a Citizens' League meeting in 1930 and lawyer and future short-term Chairman of the Girton Board, L.V. Pellew, was a prominent member of the League.[21] The members of the Adelaide Stock Exchange publicly presented as being politically neutral. Privately, it was a different matter and members, with the exception of the late Cornelius Proud, overwhelmingly supported conservative political parties. Hodgetts was true to character. He kept a low political profile, but in March 1930 when the Depression was beginning to affect South Australia, he attended the inaugural meeting of the Kensington Gardens Branch of the Political Reform League.[22] Despite its name it was far from radical. It was one of a number of liberal-democratic organisations that espoused upper- and middle-class values of independence, thrift, industry, initiative and enterprise, particularly free and private enterprise.[23] As lawyer, prominent citizen and member of the League, John Langdon

Bonython, asserted, its members 'were not suggesting anything revolutionary, but were advocating a policy of getting back to good government'.[24] In November 1935, Hodgetts' wife, Edith, hosted a committee meeting of the Kensington Garden's Women's Branch of the Liberal and Country League (LCL) at their home, Lichfield.[25] And in the 1941 federal election campaign, Hodgetts made it plain to all where his political affiliations lay when he wrote to the Editor of the *Advertiser*:

HONORING PRIME MINISTER

Sir – I have been much impressed by the manner in which large audiences at Goodwood, Mitcham, Burnside and Colonel Light Gardens received the views of the L.C.L. candidate for Boothby, Dr. Price [Archibald Grenfell Price]. It is very desirable, in the national interest, to obtain the largest possible majority for him at the forthcoming election. By bringing about this result the electors of Boothby will be supporting our Prime Minister [Robert Gordon Menzies], who has accomplished a magnificent job of work in the face of stupendous difficulties and trial. This work has been of the greatest value, not only to Australia, but to the whole Empire. – I am, Sir, &c.

H.W. HODGETTS, JUN.
40 Park Road, Kensington Park.[26]

Hodgetts' community service was devoted to maintaining the status quo. He was politically and socially conservative and opposed to radical reform. Perhaps that champion of conservatism, Edmund Burke (1729–1797), best summed it up for Hodgetts: respect for the past and the existing social system and a cautious approach to change, which should occur gradually. Governments were to eschew intellectual brilliance in favour of a clear understanding of people and common sense, and this was more likely found in those born to wealth and responsibility rather than among upwardly mobile clever people.[27]

* * *

By age 50 his father was blind and Hodgetts became an active servant of the Royal Institute for the Blind. This was especially laudable. His service to St Mark's College and Girton favoured a small, young and privileged section of the community, but this work supported people of all ages from across the social spectrum.

The Royal Institute for the Blind aimed to encourage self-help among vision-impaired people by providing training and employment. It taught brush making, basket making, mat making,

The Royal Institute for the Blind, Brougham Place, North Adelaide, c. 1909. The Institute operated from this building, originally a church, from 1884. It was demolished in 1938. (Photo: Earnest Gall. Courtesy State Library of South Australia PRG 631/2/1277)

chair caning and piano tuning. It provided a mobile library, a teacher of Braille and a pension scheme for its aged and infirm members. In 1931, it assisted 101 people and about 100 of their dependents. It was, therefore, necessary to supplement its funds through public subscription: public assistance was needed urgently. In August that year, the Institute launched an appeal to raise £10,000 and Hodgetts was the Chairman and Honorary Organiser of the Appeal Committee.[28] Hodgetts was charged with a difficult task to raise funds during the Depression, but he set about his work with dogged determination. He used his public prominence and influence to advantage and won the support of the press, which reported the progress of the appeal in painstaking detail.

Communities across the State supported the appeal in a variety of ways. After meeting personally with Hodgetts, the mayor of Burra organised a ball. Badge days were organised at a host of country shows including those at Jamestown, Naracoorte, Mount Gambier and Maitland. A women's golf gymkhana at Seaton, a concert at Loreto Convent, a dance at Wasleys and a bridge afternoon at the Henley Croquet Club all assisted the appeal. Glenelg Golf Club raised funds. A football match between Geelong and Port Adelaide was planned and there were collections at business houses and churches. Woodlands, Blanchetown Primary and Prince Alfred and St Peter's Colleges were just some of the schools to back the appeal. There was a military tattoo at Wayville Showgrounds and a concert in the Melba Theatre at Dulwich. On 4 December 1931, with Christmas approaching, only 50 of the 643 to whom the Appeal Committee sent forms had replied with promises of £63/5/11. Through the *Advertiser*, Hodgetts prodded business houses to give more generously. On 15 December 1931, the *Advertiser* reported

Hodgetts' news that the appeal had subscriptions thus far of £5077/8/7.[29] The Appeal Committee was halfway to achieving its goal in less than six months.

In early December 1938, the Institute launched the Sir John Melrose Memorial Fund to raise £5000 for a hostel at its new North Adelaide premises. Hodgetts was a member of that appeal committee too. Within three weeks the committee could be well pleased, with subscriptions worth £3659/12/-.

Hodgetts was also a member of the Institute's Committee of Management that dealt with administrative and financial matters. Despite bequests of nearly £8000, 1939 proved to be a taxing year. The Institute suffered its biggest loss since its establishment, subscriptions of £2015 were down by £74 over the previous year and the Committee expressed its gratefulness to the government, which provided a grant of £2800.[30] As well as his role in successful fundraising campaigns, Hodgetts needed to draw on his business acumen to help steer the Institute in and through troubled times. The Institute recognised the significance of Hodgetts' contribution and in September 1944 he was elected vice-president, honorary treasurer and acting honorary secretary of the organisation.[31]

* * *

Hodgetts served in other ways. During World War I, he organised a Stock Exchange Patriotic Concert that raised £70, and was a member of committees that raised funds for soldiers in France and Egypt to enjoy comforts including tobacco, chocolates, newspapers, cakes, and knitted items such as socks. At various times in the 1920s and 1930s he was a regular judge at St Peter's College's annual sports days and Chairman of its Old Collegians' Association, a committee member of the Kensington Oval Improvement Group, and a member of the Finance Committee for the 1929 League of Nations Pageant that raised funds for the Lady Victoria Buxton's Girls' Club, the League of Nations Union and the Mission to Seamen. In 1926 he joined Rotary. He was Chairman of the Executive Committee of a Flower Festival that raised £3850 in 1932 for a Tuberculosis Hostel at Angorichina in the Flinders Ranges, and in 1934 he was a member of the committee that arranged entertainment for Prince George's October visit to Adelaide.[32]

Jessie Bradman listening to the cricket at Lichfield, with her dog Robbie.
(Courtesy *Australian Women's Weekly*, 18 June 1938, p. 3)

Other members of his family served. His wife, Edith, helped at dances and fetes to raise funds for St Mary's Mission of Hope, St Mark's College, Girton and Toc H. She also invited Jessie Bradman to Lichfield to listen to broadcasts of the cricket when her husband was on tour. Daughter Mary Hodgetts was active in the Girton Old Scholars' Association and during World War II she attained the rank of lieutenant in the army and topped an anti-aircraft weapons course in Sydney. Joan, Gordon and James were involved too. The full complement of their service is unknown, but

Joan worked in the munitions factory at Salisbury, Gordon was a bombardier in the Australian Imperial Force, and James attained the rank of flying officer in the Royal Australian Air Force.[33] The Hodgetts family was imbued with the service ethic.

Hodgetts knew that all Girton headmistresses impressed upon girls the virtue of service without expectation of reward. It was, in fact, a commonly expressed ethic in all schools and promoted throughout society. Wealth, high social class and privilege carried responsibility to serve the common good, to provide the greatest good to the greatest number, free of personal financial gain. Hodgetts gave an enormous amount of his time, skill and money to serve South Australia. His service to others was unpaid, noble and altruistic. But, was he rewarded because of his voluntary work? Did it benefit his reputation, or induce investors to use H.W. Hodgetts & Co. to buy shares? It is impossible to quantify influence, to place a figure on the value that may have flowed to his business. But we know Hodgetts' conspicuous community service did not harm his business, and it may have attracted new clients.

Chapter 6

Keeping Up Appearances

Adelaide author Alison Dolling grew up in Tranmere, attended the Churches of Christ's Ellerslie Collegiate School for Girls at Magill, and worshipped at St Edward the Confessor Anglican Church, located at 16 East Terrace, Kensington Gardens. The Hodgetts family also attended St Edward's. In the early 1920s a very young Dolling sensed that Harry Hodgetts was an important man, a cut above the other congregants. In 1989, Dolling recalled, 'Mr Hodgetts impressed me by always fluttering a 10/- note into the velvet collection bag, while lesser mortals covertly dropped in 1/- or the odd threepence.'[1] In the 1920s, Hodgetts was on the make. He was what Vance Packard labelled Americans of similar inclination, a 'status seeker'.[2] He had one foot on the third- or second-highest rung of Adelaide's social ladder, the other reaching for the summit of society. And maintaining appearances was important to him.

The trappings and lifestyles of the different social classes can be identified, albeit loosely. Upper-class girls attending elite private schools such as Girton lived in grand houses in desirable locations, were practised in the 'female accomplishments', had lessons in elocution – 'A yew in a garden in Kew, Once hid a wonderful view, So they chopped down that yew-tree in Kew' – and were awarded poise badges for ladylike deportment.[3] On the other hand, a working-class lass who lived in tenement-housing in Brompton probably lacked secondary education, would have had to help her mother about the house and, when time allowed, play in the street, a virtual slum. Her older brother may have attended the trots or greyhound racing with his father, where he would have heard hearty banter delivered in an accent far removed from polished 'King's English'.

Hodgetts had assets and connections that identified him as a wealthy businessman, marginally beneath the status of the Adelaide gentry, the Adelaide Establishment. By 1927 he lived in Lichfield, a large and elegant home in a fashionable and growing suburb, Kensington Park, surrounded by remnants of an earlier idyllic rural setting. In the 1930s several Girton girls still rode horses across open paddocks on their way to school. Moreover, his wife came from old-gentry stock, his children attended Anglican private schools (*de facto* Anglican in Girton's case), and he was conspicuously prominent in enterprises connected with the Church of England, a connection with which most of the Adelaide gentry identified.

Similarly, his charitable community service and membership of the Adelaide Club allowed him to mix with the social elite. In making the 1936 Centenary Edition of *Who's Who* he was recognised as an A-lister, providing him the opportunity to rub shoulders with fellow A-listers at the exclusive Adelaide Club, including Justices Herbert Angas Parsons and Frederick Richards, John Andrew Tennant Mortlock, Senator John Duncan-Hughes, James Gosse, Edward Hawker, William Bakewell, George Morphett, MP, Victor Newland, MP, Sir Henry Simpson Newland

Henry Warburton Hodgetts Jnr, c. 1935. This portrait photograph appeared in the centenary edition of *Who's Who*.
(Courtesy *Who's Who: South Australia Centenary*, 1936, The Amalgamated Publishing Company, Adelaide, p. 198)

and Archibald Grenfell Price.[4] At St Mark's College he had close contact with the leading Anglican, his Lordship, the Bishop of Adelaide, the Right Rev. Dr Arthur Nutter Thomas, who lived near the college in Bishop's Court, North Adelaide. He was hard to miss; dressed in his black frock coat, apron, breeches and gaiters this prelate stood out among priests.[5] Working at St Mark's with Justice Thomas Poole – warden of the University of Adelaide Senate from 1922 to 1927 – and urbane classicist, Professor Henry Darnley Naylor, further enhanced Hodgetts' social reputation.[6]

As chairman of the Board of Directors of Girton Hodgetts oversaw the governance of a school with strong links to the Adelaide gentry, including the Bowman, Bonython, Rymill and Verco families, and prominent Adelaide businessmen, such as

Keeping Up Appearances

Sir Edward Holden. Sir Henry Barwell, premier of South Australia from 1920 to 1924, educated his daughters at the school and Dorothy Angove, headmistress from 1926 to 1932, had married into a prominent South Australian winemaking family.[7] A public profile was an important marker of high social status, and this required extensive coverage in the press. Hodgetts achieved this through his sporting and charitable work, while the Hodgetts family's social activities were extensively covered in the personal and social pages of the daily and weekly newspapers.

* * *

Hodgetts was out and about, catching the eye of men and women who enjoyed a privileged and comfortable lifestyle, not least the Governor of South Australia. During a Church of England Congress in October 1928, Governor Sir Alexander Hore-Ruthven invited Lieutenant-Governor Sir George Murray, Premier Richard Butler, Lord Mayor Lavington Bonython and a host of Anglican prelates and priests to lunch at Government House. As well as Bishop Nutter Thomas, the bishops of Ballarat, Carpentaria, Goulbourn, Newcastle, Riverina and Wangaratta were guests. There were two deans, five archdeacons, four canons, 12 ministers and three laymen, one of whom was the Governor's stockbroker, Henry Warburton Hodgetts Jnr.[8] In having lunch with the king's representative, a knight of the realm and seven right reverend doctors and other high Church officers Hodgetts was in prestigious company.

Harry and Edith Hodgetts were at the Adelaide Oval in July 1930 for the annual 'Intercol' football match between St Peter's and Prince Alfred Colleges. Saints won, but for the *Observer,* 'The Annual Battle Between the Blues and The Reds Was Also A Social Event' and 'Parents, Relations And Friends All Went To The Oval'.

The crowd was wonderful, exhausted eventually by its cheering and enthusiasm. The boys and girls were delightful. The Lord Mayor, the Lady Mayoress, important clergy and leading citizens attended. And,

> When a man fell or got kicked, many a mother-heart present went out in sympathy to the parents of a popular college boy who last week met with a serious accident on the football field, and is grievously ill in a private hospital. He is a fine type of sporting boy, of whom any college would be proud.[9]

These sentiments could have emanated from the playing fields of Eton, from 'home', from the 'green and pleasant land' of William Blake's England.

Hodgetts garnered social kudos from his role as a prominent South Australian and Australian cricket administrator. In November 1929, Melbourne newspaper the *Australasian* reported that Hodgetts and his wife had hosted the visiting English cricketers in their box at the *Palais Royal* at a specially arranged dance.[10] In January 1937, Adelaide's *Advertiser* noted that Mr and Mrs H.W. Hodgetts had joined the president of the SACA and his wife in entertaining the highly popular Governor, Major General Sir Winston Joseph Dugan KCMG, CB, DSO, and the glamorous Lady Dugan, in the official box during a match between South Australia and the Marylebone Cricket Club. The

Hodgetts, wearing a pith helmet, with Frank Downer at Adelaide Oval, 1932. (Courtesy *South Australian Home & Gardens*, 1 March 1932, p. 64)

Advertiser devoted the entire article to the 'White Frocks Worn By Women At Cricket', ignoring the match itself. Apparently white was the favoured colour, with Edith Hodgetts' black outfit and Mrs Don Bradman's primrose and black floral linen frock standing out from the crowd.[11]

In May 1932, Harry and Edith Hodgetts attended a Bridge Evening held in the Adelaide Town Hall to raise money for the Adelaide Branch of the English Speaking Union.[12] Founded in London in 1918, the Union promoted closer ties between English-speaking peoples around the world and aimed to develop its members' education through debating, public speaking and, today, student exchanges. The Union had grand premises, Dartmoor House in Mayfair, and at least some of its members aimed to preserve 'a quintessential Englishness, based on imperialism, class and race'.[13] In Adelaide there was a clear and obvious link between the upper and middle classes and the English Speaking Union. Empire loyalty was a keystone commitment of the upper- and middle-class Austral–Britons of that time. For them, Empire loyalty was concomitant with being Australian.

In June 1938, Hodgetts was one of 500 men who attended a levee at Government House to celebrate King George VI's birthday. All men who wished to attend were invited, but the fact that it was held on a Thursday ruled out almost all male employees, and certainly working-class men. Awareness of the niceties of upper-class behaviour and of class distinction put another brake on working-class men attending.[14] By custom, naval and military officers wore full dress, including swords, the Lord Mayor his fur-trimmed robe and chain of office, City Council members black gowns and, if they chose, Court dress with knee-length breeches and ruffles, University Councillors and graduates academic gowns and hoods, and the Chief Justice the most brilliant judicial wear, the uniform and cocked hat prescribed for Lieutenant Governors. Citizens could wear any attire, from formal morning dress and silk hat to business suits. Bowler hats, striped trousers and black coats were other favourites.[15] It would not have been a comfortable place for the *hoi polloi*. Indeed, the ceremony traced its origins via Britain to the French court of Louis XIV and the ranking of courtiers based on their relative access to the king. The masses were not welcome.[16]

The armed forces, judiciary, academia, the professions and commerce were represented at Government House on Thursday 9 June 1938. As these leading men walked the drive to the eastern doorway of Government House, guns boomed a royal salute from the adjacent parade ground. Those in the Private Entree List, who the Governor greeted personally, included the lieutenant-governor, the premier, cabinet ministers, judges, ex-ministers, naval and military commanders and heads of churches, topped, of course, by the Anglican Bishop of Adelaide. A photograph published in the *Advertiser* showed Justices Richards and Angas Parsons attending, resplendent in their judicial gowns and wigs. The Governor, Sir Winston Dugan, wore full-service dress and 'was a striking figure in his red-jacketed uniform and plumed helmet as he inspected the guard of honour on the lawns in front of Government House after the reception'. The band of the 6th Cavalry Brigade played the National Anthem and military numbers: perhaps Sir Edward Elgar's *Pomp and Circumstance* was in its repertoire.[17]

Hodgetts was in the General List, in which the names of prominent and well-connected identities abounded.[18] This placed him among Adelaide's upper classes, one step removed from those who enjoyed the closest vice-regal connection. It is likely that following the reception Hodgetts retired with fellow members

A print of Gayfield Shaw's 1938 engraving of the Adelaide Club.
(Courtesy State Library of South Australia, B 18163)

to the Adelaide Club at its prestigious North Terrace address opposite Government House to toast the King's good health. What better way to keep up appearances?

An article entitled 'Mr and Mrs H.W. Hodgetts Entertain' published in the *Advertiser* of Saturday 18 May 1935 might have sufficed. The paper reported that Harry and Edith gave a 'cheery dance' at their home for their sons T. and G. Hodgetts – Ted (Edward) and Gordon. It described how Lichfield was decorated with flowers and informed its readers of an important happening at the dance; that Miss Sydney Beresford made her social debut, no doubt enhanced by the social standing of the guests.[19] In February 1942 the *News* reported that Hodgetts' younger daughter, Joan, was one of six Girton old scholars from the Burnside district to enter the Miss Red Cross competition. The competition was essentially a fundraising activity and for this reason Hodgetts hosted a billiards party at Lichfield. What better drawcard – and what better way to catch the public eye – than a billiard match between World Billiards Champion Walter Lindrum and Don Bradman? Lindrum won. The evening raised £40, half of which was donated to the Fighting Forces Comfort Fund and half to the Red Cross. A photograph of Joan accompanied the article, further advancing the standing of the Hodgetts family.[20]

References in the press to 'Mrs H.W. Hodgetts' attending functions also helped to keep up appearances. She played a prominent part in organising the 1928 Toc H Dance at Freemasons' Hall, North Terrace.[21] In 1932 she attended Mrs E.B. Hughes' 'At Home' reception for German aviator Captain Hans Bertram, held at the Hughes family home, Athelney, in Hackney.[22] She was a member of the Lyceum Club and in 1935 attended a luncheon followed by a talk about the current state of music in Australia.[23] In 1938 she was in the official box at the Stock Exchange Ball, apparently without her husband who must have been unwell or otherwise engaged. The *Advertiser*'s 'Social Editress' noted that 700 dancers graced the floor of the *Palais Royal* and raised funds for the Adelaide Children's Hospital.[24]

Not to be outdone by 'Mrs H.W. Hodgetts' and their sisters in the social whirl of Adelaide's elite, in 1935 Ted, Gordon and James attended a dance at St Corantyn. This stately two-storey sandstone and redbrick mansion with a coach-house and servants' quarters is still situated on East Terrace, Adelaide, a desirable dress-circle location that looks over Victoria Park. This was the home of the Lord Mayor, and it was his wife, Lady Bonython, who hosted the dance for the 'younger set' of the well heeled and well known. There was always the chance that one of the Hodgetts lads might catch the eye of a damsel from one of Adelaide's leading families.[25]

Chapter 7

The Road to Ruin

Following the collapse of H.W. Hodgetts & Co. on 2 June 1945, the Official Receiver, G.W. Burns, examined its financial affairs. Subsequently, Hodgetts endured public examination in the Bankruptcy Court. Hodgetts claimed to have flourished until the Great Depression, but that in about 1930 he suffered a 'bad knock' when his Broken Hill agent defaulted, committed suicide and left him a loss of £10,000. Burns contended that Hodgetts had overestimated the extent of his loss.[1]

In 1996 Professor Roland Perry wrote that Hodgetts' Broken Hill agent misappropriated clients' funds in 1942. In 2019, Perry changed the date to 1941. Putting aside discrepancies over the date for the moment, Perry suggested that it was this agent's crime that pushed Hodgetts towards insolvency, caused him to panic and to use investors' funds to cover his losses.[2] To Perry this was the tipping point in Hodgetts' demise. It is plausible, but not true. Hodgetts' account of events in Broken Hill, their timing and their consequences, was more reliable, although he may have overstated its effect on his long-term financial position.

* * *

Allan Edward Hall was Hodgetts' Broken Hill agent. Born about 1889, he worked in his father's real estate agency from 1908 until 1918 when he and his father formed a partnership and traded under the name of 'T. Hall and Son'. In 1924 the company ventured into sharebroking, with the *Barrier Miner* reporting that a member of the firm made frequent visits to Adelaide to keep up with the latest news. That visitor was Allan Hall and he met with Hodgetts to keep abreast of trading trends.[3] Hall became Hodgetts' agent. But the speculative Hall wanted more. He was one of six Broken Hill men who formed a syndicate to mine for gold at Mount Magnet, about 560 kilometres north-north-east of Perth in Western Australia. In August 1927 Hall visited the claim and interviewed the West Australian Minister for Mines with a view to obtaining a State-funded battery for the mine.[4] Hall was then a member of the Broken Hill Hospital Board of Management and secretary of the Broken Hill Chamber of Commerce. Within the year Hall's father had died, and by September 1928 he was negotiating to sell the business and manage a new company – Home Sanitation Ltd – in Melbourne.[5] Hall had killed his father's business in just four years after he began trading on the stock market.

Worse was to come. On 13 March 1929, the 39-year-old Hall was charged with false pretences. It was alleged in the Broken Hill Police Court that on 15 June 1928 he had falsely advised client S.W. Heuzenroeder that he had purchased 300 Broken Hill South and 300 Zinc Corporation shares for him, together valued at £200. The case was adjourned until 27 March and given the possibility of further charges involving more than £2000, bail was fixed with a surety of £400.[6] Failing to appear at the adjourned court proceedings, that same day Hall committed suicide near an old house that he owned on the outskirts of Broken Hill. He left behind his widow, a 12-year-old son and two younger daughters, and a note that read, 'Florrie, don't forget the insurances are yours and the kiddies. Love. – Allan. 27/3/29'.[7]

The full extent of his misappropriation is uncertain, but 26 proofs of debt were submitted at a meeting of creditors in September 1930. Richard Johnson of Broken Hill was owed £458, but the not-for-profit co-operative, the Starr-Bowkett Society, was the largest creditor.[8] The extent to which Hall's misappropriation of funds affected H.W. Hodgetts & Co. is unknown, but creditor John Thomas Gorman's decision to pursue legal action exacerbated Hodgetts' 'bad knock'.

Gorman had been a warder at Broken Hill Gaol and in June 1926 he entrusted his life savings with Hall and asked him to purchase shares on his behalf. Hall passed instructions on to Hodgetts and the fact that Gorman was his client. When Hall defaulted Gorman lost £1740. To seek recompense, in November 1932 before Mr Justice Angas Parsons in Adelaide's Civil

'Verdict for J.T. Gorman', (*Barrier Miner*, 16 December 1932, p. 1)

Justice Herbert Angas Parsons, the Civil Court judge who ruled against Hodgetts in the J.T. Gorman case.
(Courtesy *Who's Who: South Australia Centenary*, 1936)

Court, Gorman sought an account from H.W. Hodgetts & Co. in respect of Zinc Corporation and other shares and damages for the alleged sale and conversion of the shares. Gorman claimed that Hodgetts had refused to pay him the proceeds from the sale of the shares. Hodgetts denied the allegations, arguing that he believed that he had bought shares on behalf of T. Hall and Son, adding that he had paid Hall all money owing in respect of the shares.

The parties' Counsels agreed that the matter arose out of the default of a third party and that one of the innocent parties – the plaintiff Gorman or the defendant Hodgetts – must suffer the cost. Angas Parsons reserved judgment and reviewed the relevant share transactions.[9] On 16 December 1932, Angas Parsons handed down his judgment, concluding that on this occasion Hodgetts was acting as Hall's agent. The Judge said, 'It was clear that Hodgetts had no right to sell Gorman's shares in the absence of an expressed or implied authority from Gorman.' Angas Parsons ordered Hodgetts to pay Gorman £1740 – a sum just over eight times the average male national income – and costs.[10]

It appears that at some time between June 1926 and September 1928 a desperate Hall instructed Hodgetts to sell Gorman's shares, without his client's consent or knowledge. By 1928, if not before, Hall had resorted to illegal practices in an attempt to trade his way out of financial difficulty. Among other fraudulent practices he cashed in Gorman's shares to pay other clients. It is possible, but far from certain, that Hodgetts told Hall that this was a practice to which brokers resorted to get through difficult times. It is just as likely that Hall kept his shameful misdeeds to himself and, like Gorman, Hodgetts was unaware of Hall's deceit.

Angas Parsons' decision hurt Hodgetts badly, especially given the latter's claim to have already paid Hall the money from the sale of the shares. If this were true, Hodgetts paid up twice. But it was not the tipping point that ruined Hodgetts. We shall see later that he could not claim that Hall's default and suicide was the only – nor the main – cause of his failure. But in 1932 the Depression was still biting and Hodgetts' trading commission was reduced in 1933 from 6·5 per cent to 5·75 per cent at the very time he was trying to recover from the payout to Gorman, a sum significantly less than the £10,000 he claimed to have lost. How much Hodgetts lost is unknown, but it is likely that he suffered other losses at Hall's hand. Hodgetts claimed to have lost between £10,000 and £15,000 between 1929 and 1934.[11]

* * *

In the mid-1930s Hodgetts gambled in a highly speculative practice and took on a new client. The first of these steps sowed the seed of his downfall; the second was to trigger it.

From 1936 Hodgetts began trading in wheat certificates, or 'wheat futures'.[12] A bumper wheat crop in 1915/1916 and an acute shortage of shipping caused by World War I had produced serious problems for farmers. In response, the federal government created the Australian Wheat Board, which set up a wheat pool. The Board issued growers wheat certificates as advances on wheat delivered to the pool. The certificates could be used as security for bank loans, or they could be traded before being redeemed. Farmers, however, complained about slow payments and, along with other Australian exchanges, the Stock Exchange of Adelaide listed them for trade in June 1917. By 1918, this was a lucrative source of income and many brokers traded the certificates profitably. But, trading in wheat certificates attracted speculators, especially when heavy falls followed problems with selling the balance of crops held in the wheat pools.[13]

Trading on his own behalf, Hodgetts saw this as a way out of

Left: Sir Alexander Hore-Ruthven, posing here with koalas, demanded Hodgetts realise his scrip in 1944. (*Courtesy South Australian Homes & Gardens*, 1 June 1934, p. 6) *Right:* Lady Zara Hore-Ruthven, in the uniform of the Girl Guides.
(*Courtesy South Australian Homes & Gardens*, 2 April 1934, p. 2)

his current financial difficulties. He speculated in wheat futures between 1936 and 1939, a gamble that did not pay dividends. He lost heavily. Exactly how much he lost is unknown as his bookkeeping was highly irregular. He constructed fictitious accounts to hide his losses. He named a bogus client account 'N. Cash' to hide a loss of £6558/10/7, which represented a portion of his losses in wheat-futures gambling over four years. Another account of £6850 was also suspect. It included losses almost certainly accrued this way. He also adopted the dangerous practice of using clients' accounts in this speculative dealing, unbeknown to them.[14] By 1939, the Union Bank was pressing him over his overdrawn account.[15]

Meanwhile, in 1937 Hodgetts handled a large investment for an important client. During Hodgetts' trial the *Advertiser* referred to the client as a 'gentleman', rather than by name. The 'gentleman' was Lord Gowrie, the Governor-General of Australia. Being broker to Lord Gowrie, and Lady Gowrie, brought social prestige that Adelaide's most high-profile sharebroker found impossible to resist, even at the time he had begun gambling in wheat futures. Gowrie had known Hodgetts when he, as Sir Alexander Hore Ruthven, served as South Australia's governor from 1928 until 1934. Lord Gowrie invested £12,600 and Lady Gowrie £2000 with Hodgetts.[16] These very substantial investments represented temptation that Hodgetts was unable to resist some eight years later. Indeed, when his business collapsed in June 1945, Hodgetts' grand home, Lichfield, was valued at £8000, £6600 less than Lord and Lady Gowrie's original investments.

The effects of Hall's default and his own gambling on wheat futures set Hodgetts on the downward spiral to ruin. He knew that he was in trouble by June 1940, and taking on Lord and Lady Gowrie's portfolio was to prove critical in his eventual downfall.[17]

Chapter 8

Financial Folly and Failure

Hodgetts was on shaky ground by 1940, but several events in the next four years – within and without his control – saw him adopt foolhardy and fraudulent business practices based on an over-optimistic self-belief in his capacity to trade out of trouble. He had accumulated bad debts, war restrictions undermined the stockbroking business in general, and his cash flow had halved.[1] Hopelessness drove a despairing Hodgetts to desperately dangerous measures. They failed to save him.

* * *

In 1939, £2.5 million passed through H.W. Hodgetts & Co.'s books, but it was barely solvent. Hodgetts had an overdraft of £50,000 and with clients financed to the extent of £55,000 he faced a serious dilemma.[2] In July 1938 Hodgetts had to finance clients to the extent of £7453 and his 1939 interest bill on moneys borrowed was a staggering £9395.[3] As well as carrying a heavy overdraft with the Union Bank, in June 1940 Hodgetts owed Alexander Melrose £9800. Long-established clients such as Mr H.N. Neill and Sir Wallace Sandford knew that Hodgetts was in trouble, but only

Melrose helped him out financially. Hodgetts preferred it that way as he thought he could 'get through' with the help of one friend.[4]

A bespectacled, quiet and retiring bachelor, Melrose was a solicitor, writer and patron of the arts. A descendant of the old-gentry pastoralist George Melrose (1806–1894), he was also a generous benefactor. In 1934 he gave £10,000 for extensions to the National Gallery of South Australia. When he died in September 1944 his estate was sworn for probate at £279,906. Melrose was a member of the Adelaide Club and one-time president of the South Australian Branch of the Royal Institute for the Blind, both institutions of which Hodgetts was also a member.[5] They became friends and Melrose helped Hodgetts to hang on for several years.

As we saw in Chapter 2, in 1940 Hodgetts joined with William Lapthorne, Maurice Smith and Adelaide hotelier Arthur Lee to buy and develop Darwin's two hotels.[6] Confidence in the bricks-and-mortar project was high and it promised a more reliable return than that from investing in 'futures' on the market. Hodgetts underwrote 42,225 Hotel Darwin shares, valued at £5238.[7] What could possibly go wrong? On 19 February 1942 the Japanese bombed Darwin and the syndicate's investment was smashed, literally. Hodgetts lost his £5238. On top of that, in 1942 Hodgetts' largest investor, solicitor Guy Fisher, first sought recompense for covering his securities. From about 1943 to 1945 Fisher continuously pressed Hodgetts to return his scrip.[8] Pressure was mounting. What other legal and less-risky measures could Hodgetts pursue?

* * *

Hodgetts was a political conservative who supported the re-election of the Menzies Government during the 1941 federal election. He feared the imposition of war restrictions under a

Labor Government led by John Curtin. His worst fears were realised when Labor won the election and Curtin became Prime Minister. As part of an emergency package of measures to defend Australia against a potential Japanese invasion, the incoming government prohibited the sale of investment capital, except for war purposes such as the buying of war bonds. It also fixed interest rates. Stock exchanges were dismayed and the Melbourne and Adelaide Exchanges shared their concerns. When Singapore fell to the Japanese on 15 February 1942 alarm bells rang throughout Australia, not least in regard to business matters.[9] Four days later Japanese bombs shattered Hodgetts' Darwin investments.

Hodgetts had more to fear than other brokers, fears he could not reveal. Restrictions on his capacity to trade may account for him involving himself directly in the broader affairs of the Stock Exchange. In February, key brokers Andrew Young and Cuthbert Viner Smith had attended a Chamber of Commerce meeting that telegrammed the Prime Minister urging him to delay the planned controls until further consultation could be had. In March, Hodgetts visited Canberra to lobby for amendments. Several weeks later, he returned with Gordon Sunter to lobby against the government's new regulations.[10] His problems may also have motivated his offer to represent the Exchange in a delegation to meet the federal Treasurer and to stand, successfully, in early 1943 for election to the Exchange Committee.[11]

Despite the lobbying, Curtin placed the war effort first and wartime controls over stock trading persisted. Hodgetts' only hope lay with an economic boom that would allow him to restore clients' funds without anyone being the wiser, but boom years were impossible during World War II and its end came too late for Hodgetts to trade legally out of his dilemma.[12] Before financial folly took over, Hodgetts reduced his expenditure. Between 1935 and 1940 he had provided Edith an annual allowance of £1400, which he reduced in 1940 to £1200. In 1941 he reduced it to £600. He had allowed himself £10 a week, or £520 a year. Hodgetts paid on average £550 a year on life insurance policies.[13] These payments would have amazed and dismayed working-class families in Bowden, Brompton and elsewhere, and Hodgetts' future creditors.

* * *

With Fisher persisting with his demands that he repay him, Hodgetts stepped over the brink of legal practice into trading madness. Overdrawn at the bank, Hodgetts had earlier turned to Fisher for help; at 7 per cent interest, when the bank rate was 5 per cent. Hodgetts admitted that there was no way that he could 'liberate the whole of that scrip since 1940 through his own resources' and so he used dividends paid on other clients' shares to pay Fisher every six months.[14] Hodgetts gave to Fisher with one hand and took from him with the other. For example, in February 1942 he cashed up 1000 of Fisher's South Australian Brush Company shares as extra cover for Melrose's account. In July 1943 he pledged Melrose 5400 of Fisher's Sands & McDougall shares against his recent advance of £5000. He also pledged Melrose 1100 of Fisher's shares in the Fijian gold mine Loloma. Hodgetts later admitted that Fisher had no idea that he had placed his scrip with others. In desperation, Hodgetts even pledged Melrose his own Adelaide Club debentures, valued at £200.[15]

Hodgetts lost his main supporter when Melrose died on 2 September 1944, just weeks before Lord Gowrie asked him to realise his scrip of about £13,000. Hodgetts stalled, but when Gowrie left to return to the United Kingdom at the end of the year, he pressed for a full and final settlement. Hodgetts was unable to obtain the last £6000 he owed Gowrie. To this end, he borrowed £3500 from another broker and £2800 from the Bank of Adelaide.[16]

To obtain the loan from the Bank of Adelaide Hodgetts resorted to deceit. He told its General Manager, Oscar Isaachsen, that he needed money to cover an overseas debt and that having reached the limit of his overdraft the Union Bank had refused him an advance. Hodgetts owed the Union Bank about £19,000 secured by a £16,000 life insurance policy – the surrender value of which was £6800, £1500 on his home and industrial and mining shares. He told Isaachsen, however, that while his liabilities were £28,000, he was owed £40,000, of which he thought about 80 per cent could be relied upon. This satisfied Isaachsen, and on Tuesday 22 May 1945, he granted a temporary advance of £2800 without security, but on the condition that it be repaid by the following Monday. Under cross-examination in the Bankruptcy Court on 17 August 1945, Isaachsen admitted that he would not have made the advance if he had known the real situation: that Hodgetts' deficit was in the region of £80,000.[17] This loan was granted about a week and a half before Hodgetts voluntarily declared himself bankrupt, and the *West Australian* claimed that this was what tipped him over the abyss.[18] But there was more to it than that. In September 1944, Hodgetts had been appointed honorary treasurer and secretary of the Royal Institute for the Blind, both positions reflecting the unquestioned trust in which the institute held him.[19] We shall see in Chapter 9 that Hodgetts abused this trust the very day before he admitted that he could no longer meet his obligations.

As well as trading insolvent, Hodgetts resorted to deceitful accounting practices to mislead, and to hide his real position. At the time he was bankrupted he had not written off bad debts for the previous nine years. At the end of each year, he transferred the balance of his profit and loss account to his drawing account. On 1 September 1935 that account alone had a debit balance of £416. That had risen until on 2 June 1945 it was £34,380. Hodgetts' losses on stock exchange transactions that had never been written off totalled £2168/11/8. Official Receiver Burns found that Hodgetts had prepared 'balance sheets' for the Union Bank. The last one was headed 'Balance-sheet as at March 13 1945', and designed to mislead the bank: it showed a surplus of assets over liabilities, yet Hodgetts' June statement of accounts showed a total debit of £82,854.[20] His deceit was complete.

Burns summarised the practices that Hodgetts had used to finance his business. These were:

1. Borrowing on overdraft from the Union Bank, depositing scrip in some instances the property of clients as security for the advance,
2. Borrowing from other brokers and friends and giving as security in many instances scrip which was the property of clients,
3. Accepting money on call from clients and, in some instances, furnishing other clients' scrip as security,
4. Borrowing scrip from clients to use as security for money advanced [and]
5. Using scrip deposited with the bankrupt [Hodgetts] or friends who had also given him a power of attorney.[21]

Burns concluded that by the time of his bankruptcy, Hodgetts had used for security on cash advances almost every negotiable share held in his office.[22]

Financial Folly and Failure

* * *

On Saturday 2 June 1945, Vice-President Viner Smith shocked the Stock Exchange of Adelaide by announcing at morning call that Hodgetts could no longer meet his commitments. Viner Smith added that Hodgetts had petitioned for bankruptcy. The Exchange Committee met and suspended Hodgetts' membership. Bradman had bought a seat on the Exchange in May 1943 but continued to work as Hodgetts' clerk, so Viner Smith allowed him to explain to the Exchange that he was not a partner in – and had no financial interest in – Hodgetts' company.[23] The order to sequestrate Hodgetts' estate was made at noon. His lawyer, Mr William Norman, said that the order was made at that time to protect creditors and to enable the Official Receiver to investigate the position. Norman advised creditors that the Receiver would accept their claims as soon as possible.[24] Worn down and in ill health, Hodgetts was in desperate straits, knowing that his shame was soon to be revealed in full and frank detail.

Chapter 9

Public Shame

News of Hodgetts' bankruptcy spread rapidly, immediately by word of mouth from those in the know and through the press from Monday 4 June. Attention focused on what the creditors could expect to receive once H.W. Hodgetts & Co. was liquidated.[1] Creditors had good reason to be concerned, as did other brokers, the Stock Exchange, the South Australian Parliament, and the general public. Hodgetts had rocked faith in stockbroking and investing on the stock market. The Stock Exchange went into damage control. On Tuesday 5 June, the *Advertiser* reported that 'Mr. Don Bradman [was] In Business On His Own' as a stockbroker.[2] Meanwhile Hodgetts, afflicted with painful rheumatic gout, confined himself to his sick bed at Lichfield to await developments. Shortly after the Official Receiver had examined the company's books the Bankruptcy Court conducted a public examination of Hodgetts' financial position and, subsequently, he was sent to trial and to gaol.

* * *

Stock Exchange President Andrew Young was in Melbourne on Saturday 2 June 1945 and when he learned the news of Hodgetts' collapse that morning, he returned to Adelaide the following day. As Adelaideans read the news on page two of the Monday *Advertiser*, Young met with Viner Smith, Official Receiver Burns and Bradman to discuss how best to clear up the accounts of Hodgetts' clients. Burns allowed Bradman to register a new business – Don Bradman & Co. – and begin trading that afternoon. Bradman set up in Hodgetts' fully furnished office and was allowed to access the former company's client list. The *Advertiser* observed that it normally took a month for the Receiver to determine whether a company could trade its way out of its difficulties.[3] The Stock Exchange was keen to limit damage to its reputation and standing in business circles, but what appeared to be its favoured treatment of Bradman raised eyebrows and questions.

Andrew Young, President, Stock Exchange of Adelaide, at the time of Hodgetts' failure.
(Courtesy *Who's Who: South Australia Centenary*, 1936)

Burns examined the company's books in June and lodged his first report in the Bankruptcy Court on 11 July. Hodgetts' books were the usual ones and they had been well kept, but they did not show his true financial position in the five years before sequestration. As well as exposing Hodgetts' deceit and fraudulent accounting practices, Burns revealed Hodgetts' claim that he had followed a recognised and customary stockbroking practice: the unauthorised use of clients' scrip for finance purposes where the client's account was in debt, even to the extent of only £1 or so. Burns noted that in many instances Hodgetts had pledged the scrip of clients who were not in debt and that he had deducted 'carrying charges' from their accounts. Burns determined that a system that allowed Hodgetts to act in these ways, and to deposit securities without the authority to do so, was seriously flawed.[4] He concluded:

> the bankrupt's financial difficulties are largely attributable to the fact that for a number of years he has been operating entirely on borrowed money and was financing clients when he could ill afford the accommodation. The books of account were never subject to audit and although profit and loss accounts were prepared annually no balance sheets were incorporated in the books showing the position of the bankrupt at the end of each trading period.[5]

While Burns did not attempt to whitewash Hodgetts' fraudulent and deceitful practices, he looked beyond his flaws and suggested that others must bear some responsibility for what had happened under their watch. He wrote:

> As far as I am aware, there is no statutory control, such as a periodical audit by competent investigators over brokers, who deal with large amounts of investors' moneys, and there is not even any provision for the keeping of a trust account for the receipt of moneys held specifically on behalf of clients for special purposes.
>
> The position whereby [the] bankrupt was able to use trust moneys for his own ends, for a time, appears to require the attention of the governing bodies in order to safeguard clients against the possibility of losses.[6]

Within several days of Hodgetts' bankruptcy news breaking, South Australian Premier, Thomas Playford, advised Young and Viner Smith that his government would introduce legislation requiring the compulsory audit of sharebrokers' books. The Exchange reacted immediately. It released a statement to the press denying that sharebrokers commonly used clients' scrip without their authority. It informed its members that licensed auditors would examine their books for the preceding year and hereafter they would be audited annually.[7] Damage control was in full swing.

When Burns examined the books, he found that there were 238 unsecured creditors and a deficit of £82,854/8/11. Total assets were £31,854/8/1, with a contingent asset of £900, which represented two seats on the Stock Exchange. Liabilities listed for dividend amounted to £114,933/17/6. There were some very large unsecured creditors who were prominent in Adelaide business and sporting circles, and polite society. Hodgetts owed Guy Fisher £34,576; cricketer Arthur Richardson £8093; Mr J.R. Tobin, £5947; Mr H.W. Reid £5516; Mrs L.M.A. Hughes £4818; the Bank of Adelaide £2783; Mrs D.B.C. Dolling £1807; Mrs A. Hawker £1470; Mr David Hawker £1095; H.W. Hodgetts Trust Account (E. Hodgetts) £2581; Mrs R. Levinge £1185 and Miss L.A.E. Peacock £1011. Mrs E.M. Chomley of North Bungaree (£788/15/-) and Don Bradman (£762) were among the creditors owed less than £1000. There were creditors secured to the amount of £59,863, including the Union Bank and the Melrose estate, so prospects for the unsecured creditors were decidedly bleak.[8] It is no wonder that Hodgetts had confined himself to bed.

* * *

On the morning of Saturday 14 July, Detectives Strangway and Packham of the South Australian Police Force interviewed and arrested Hodgetts at Lichfield. Sick and still in bed at the time of his arrest, he dressed and accompanied the detectives to the City

'Arrested Man At Court' (*News*, 14 July 1945, p. 1)

Watch House. At 11 am he was arraigned in No. 1 Police Court, Victoria Square. He was in severe pain. His wife assisted him into the court and his lawyer, William Norman, helped him into the dock. The *News* reported: 'Hodgetts today as he stood in the dock was a vastly different figure from the active businessman he was a few months ago. His mop of iron-grey hair and tired features gave him the appearance of a sick man.' Only three charges were laid and the proceedings took 10 minutes. In asking for bail, Norman said that Hodgetts would attend his trial as he could have absconded already had he wanted, and because he was a sick man. Bail was set at £1000 in his own bond and two sureties of £500 each.[9]

Less than a month later, on Monday 6 August, Hodgetts first appeared before the Bankruptcy Court for public examination. The examination revealed all. Nothing was spared. Mr F.V. Smith,

KC, acting for main creditor Guy Fisher, cross-examined Hodgetts. When referring to the help he had received from Melrose, Hodgetts became tearful and Smith suggested that he try to remain calm. Hodgetts replied, 'I am keeping calm, and trying to render all the help I can.'

Smith was candid, telling Hodgetts at one stage, 'I am trying to repair some of the severe loss on the man who, through no fault of his own, has lost about £35,000.' Smith pressed Hodgetts hard, pointing out that he had deliberately 'applied' 2000 shares belonging to Fisher 'within six weeks of sequestration, with nothing more than hope'. Hodgetts explained that he had sold some of Fisher's T.J. Richards Motor Body shares in March and April and was instructed to buy North Broken Hill shares with the proceeds, worth £10,800. Hodgetts received the money in cash and paid it into his own account at the Union Bank. Smith then said, 'Your records show that on May 23, under pressure from the bank, you misappropriated Mr Fisher's shares by having the transfer entered in your own name, contrary to the instructions of the true owner.' Hodgetts objected to Smith using the term 'misappropriated', consulted Norman and on his advice refused to answer the question on the ground that it might incriminate him. Registrar Forbes called for the Bankruptcy Court Judge, Herbert Paine, to make a ruling. Paine consulted with Smith and Norman who agreed on the form the question should take. After Paine retired, Smith asked Hodgetts, 'Did you transfer Mr Fisher's shares to your own name, contrary to his instructions?'

Hodgetts replied, 'Yes.'[10]

The Melbourne *Herald* made sure that its readers gleaned direct insight into what Hodgetts had been doing. It reported passages verbatim, including the following:

[Hodgetts read out a list of financial transactions between 1936 and the date of sequestration, June 2 1945.]

Mr Smith: When you pledged each of these parcels you were insolvent? – I was solvent in 1936.

Mr Smith: In April 1945, you knew your position was hopeless? – I knew it was very, very bad.

And:

[He (Hodgetts) assigned Mr Melrose four Adelaide Club debentures worth £200. As a member he was bound to have only one debenture, but he had four.]

Mr Smith: You had no delicacy about pawning your club debentures? – Not a bit.

And:

Mr Smith: When you handed over 1,000 SA Brush Company shares to Mr Neill on April 10, 1945, didn't you know you were parting with Mr Fisher's securities beyond all hope of redeeming them? – I had hope.

Mr Smith: Apart from Neill, how many members of the public outside the Stock Exchange did you have depositing with you, with securities in positions parallel to Mr Neill? – Half a dozen at the most.

Mr Smith – Did Mr Fisher know that 1,100 Lolomas were in the hands of Neill? – He did not know where I pledged his scrip.

Mr Smith – Did you tell Mr Neill of your financial resources when you set up in business? – No.[11]

The press reported 'The Hodgetts Affair' throughout South Australia and the country. Regional papers gave succinct accounts, while the city papers divulged Hodgetts' folly in full. It was there for all to see. At the end of the first day's proceedings, Hodgetts took the opportunity to say, 'I am very sorry for all my clients and friends and for everyone who has lost money through my failure. That has been the cause of my illness. I have been wanting to say that.'[12]

Two men who could shed at least a little light on Hodgetts' dealings were also cross-examined in the Bankruptcy Court. One was Oscar Isaachsen, General Manager of the Bank of Adelaide. When Mr E. Phillips, acting for the Official Receiver, questioned Isaachsen in the Bankruptcy Court on 17 August, Hodgetts' deliberate deception of the Bank was writ large in the local press.[13] And, if that were not enough to set tongues wagging, on Monday 27 August Phillips examined Mr Edward Yule, Lord and Lady Gowrie's agent.

Yule had first dealt with Hodgetts on 28 September 1944. Under Phillips' questioning, Yule revealed that Hodgetts had held considerable scrip and securities under his own name as trustee for 'Their Excellencies', and that he had told Hodgetts that they now wanted their investments realised and the proceeds banked for transfer to the Governor-General's account. Hodgetts had replied that he would pay in 'evens': even thousands of pounds, as they were 'cleaner'. Accordingly, Hodgetts paid £2000 in a first payment, £635 short of the sale total. Moreover, Yule was unaware that Hodgetts had realised up to £5000 worth of Lord and Lady Gowrie's stock. Hodgetts promised a final settlement on 15 May, but then asked for more time as 'he was a little out of practice in attending to detailed work'.[14] Hodgetts repaid almost all of the outstanding money – part borrowed and part acquired by deceiving the Bank of Adelaide, but nevertheless he swindled the country's Governor-General of £257.[15]

On the same day that Phillips cross-examined Yule, Hodgetts appeared before Mr George Ziesing, SM, in the Adelaide Police Court. Ziesing concluded that it was likely that Hodgetts would be summonsed directly to the Supreme Court. He cancelled proceedings and remanded Hodgetts for another 14 days, until 10 September.[16]

* * *

On Friday 7 September 1945, Hodgetts appeared before Justice Frederick Richards in the Supreme Court charged with four counts of fraud and one of false pretences. The prosecution relied on charges that would stand up against vigorous cross-examination. These charges were that Hodgetts fraudulently converted for his own use:

> about May 11, 1945, scrip for 570 shares in Broken Hill South Ltd., valued at £800, entrusted to him by Ella Mildred Chomley to hold in safe custody for Marion Farr;
>
> on June 1 a cheque for £5,000 entrusted to him by the Institute for the Blind Inc. to invest for it in a Commonwealth Loan;
>
> on various dates in and since 1941, scrip for 200 shares in the SA Brewing Co. Ltd., 500 in Woolworths Ltd., 400 in Goldsborough Mort & Co. Ltd., 300 in Advertiser Newspapers Ltd., 250 in Felt & Textiles Ltd., and 400 in Broken Hill South Ltd., of a total value

Justice Frederick William Richards, in 1935, was the Supreme Court judge who sent Hodgetts to gaol. (Courtesy State Library of South Australia, B 6797) of about £3,680, and £320 in money received by him on account of Hugh Wesley Reid;

during March 1945 Commonwealth War Loan Bonds valued at £900 received on account of Hugh Wesley Reid:

and that at Adelaide on May 22, 1945, with intent to defraud caused £2,800 to be paid for his use and benefit by the Bank of Adelaide Ltd., by falsely pretending that the value of his assets exceeded his liabilities and that his financial position was such that he would be able to repay the said money on May 28, 1945.[17]

Crown Prosecutor R.R. Chamberlain advised the court that after Hodgetts' estate had been sequestrated, his solicitor had handed the Royal Institute for the Blind's solicitor a transfer of stock for £5000 by way of restitution and later the interest was paid. Mrs Hodgetts had signed the transfer.[18] At least Hodgetts repaid the blind, from whom he had stolen.

Hodgetts pleaded guilty and his counsel, Mr J.W. Nelligan, pleaded for leniency. Nelligan argued that Hodgetts had never set out to rob anyone and that an incurable optimism had caused his catastrophe. This optimism, Nelligan said, 'drove him on until he was at last caught in the cross currents of changing economic circumstances and blinded by that optimism he went down.' Nelligan pointed out Hodgetts' age and that he had five children, one serving in the AIF, another in the RAAF, and that his two daughters were doing their bit in the women's services. Nelligan reminded the court that Hodgetts had voluntarily petitioned for sequestration and submitted that his client's sentence should not be crushing and he hoped that it would give him the opportunity to atone and to redeem himself.[19]

Justice Richards ordered Hodgetts be held in custody and

'Defrauder, In Gaol, Awaits Sentence' (*Truth*, 9 September 1945, p. 15)

adjourned proceedings to consider his sentence over the weekend. *Truth's* Adelaide office despatched the news around the country with the headline: 'Defrauder, In Gaol, Awaits Sentence'. It opened its item in sensational fashion:

> From his palatial two-storey Kensington Park home to the cold cells of Adelaide Gaol may seem a tragic step for this

big shot, who had been on the Australian Board of Control of International Cricket and president of the South Australia [sic] Olympic Council, until it is considered that perhaps some of his large clientele too are suffering many of the discomforts of life as a result of Hodgetts' manipulations.[20]

On Monday 10 September, Richards pronounced his sentence. He was thankful that Hodgetts had pleaded guilty, thereby saving the expense of proving or disproving the charges to the satisfaction of a jury. A member of the Adelaide Club, Richards told his fellow member Hodgetts: 'You will believe me when I say that this is one of the most unwelcome of the duties which have fallen my lot during nearly 21 years on this Bench.' Richards agreed with Nelligan that Hodgetts' crime was not predetermined, but that he succumbed to temptation in the face of a disastrous combination of embarrassing difficulties. Richards was swayed by Nelligan's appeal for some leniency and a sentence that would allow Hodgetts to recover his self-respect. But the crime called for a heavy sentence. Richards sentenced Hodgetts to five years gaol for each of the four fraud charges and three years for the false pretences charge. Hodgetts was to serve all charges concurrently. The *News* pointed out that he would receive a 10-month War Victory remission that the Commonwealth Government had recently introduced. If he behaved well in prison the remaining 50 months would be reduced by a third. If so, he would have to serve about 33 months. As a first offender he was entitled to apply for release on probation when he had served half his sentence.[21] It was possible that he could be released after 17 months. Hodgetts burst into tears as he left the dock and a constable had to assist him down a step to his cell.[22] Hodgetts was incarcerated in Yatala Labour Prison.

Chapter 10

Fallout

The revelation of Hodgetts' bankruptcy and the illegal practices he had used sent shock waves throughout Adelaide, South Australia and the entire country. It had profound short- and long-term effects on individuals closely affected by the scandal, the Stock Exchange of Adelaide and other brokers, and public trust in business and legislation. Historian Brett Hutchins called it the biggest financial scandal in South Australian history to that time.[1] In *The Private Lives of Australian Cricket Stars*, R.M. Patching compared average weekly earnings in 1945 to those in 2013 to indicate the size of Hodgetts' financial collapse. He suggested that Hodgetts' losses equated in 2013 to about 205 years' annual income of a 1945 average-wage-earner, and roughly equated to $11,800,000.[2] No wonder there was disquiet.

* * *

As we saw in Chapter 9, the Playford Government responded quickly and oversaw the passage of a Bill to introduce regulations to control the stockbroking industry. For some years there had been disquiet in business circles that sharebrokers were not subjected to the same audit requirements that applied to lawyers' trust funds. The collapse of sharebrokers Edward Ward & Co. in Melbourne in 1937 had been as sensational as Hodgetts' failure, and it had prompted the Victorian Parliament to pass legislation. The Playford Government used the Victorian legislation as its model and the South Australian Parliament subsequently passed a Bill requiring the auditing of brokers' books, open accounts for clients' funds, and the keeping of proper books and accounts.[3]

Debate in the House of Assembly sheeted home the need for legislation to Hodgetts: the 'Hodgetts case', as politicians called it, was the catalyst for reforming and regulating stockbroking. Based on Victoria's experience, Attorney-General Charles Abbott concluded that compulsory audits were an effective safeguard and added, 'had Hodgetts known that his accounts were to be audited, the amount (sic) of defalcations would have been much smaller'. In responding to a question about the efficacy of the proposed legislation, among other things, Abbott stated that 'you cannot stop a crook from being a crook'. Discussion raised issues such as licensing brokers, the public's right to know that only the 'right type of person' was licensed, and that under the new legislation brokers would be allowed only one trust account.[4]

In Federal Parliament, Labor Member for Adelaide Cyril Chambers questioned the banks' compliance with government regulations in respect of their dealings with the fraudulent Hodgetts. On 18 July 1945, in the House of Representatives, Chambers asked a Dorothy Dix question:

> Will the Treasurer inform the House whether the unsecured advance made by the Bank of Adelaide to W.H. [sic] Hodgetts,

sharebroker, of Adelaide, complied with the policy with regard to advances laid down by the Commonwealth Bank in accordance with National Security Regulations? If that policy does not cover such advances will it be amended accordingly? Under the new banking legislation, will the Treasurer ensure that banks shall not be permitted to make advances to customers on the security of scrip to which the customers have no title, such as the advances made by the Union Bank of Australia Limited to W.H. [sic] Hodgetts.[5]

Ben Chifley, the newly elected Prime Minister and former Treasurer in the Curtin Government, rose to speak.[6] He made it clear that the granting of advances on security of scrip not belonging to brokers had caused him concern for some time and that the Hodgetts case had focused his attention on the issue. He defended the banks. They could not have known, he asserted, that the scrip offered as security was not Hodgetts' property. Hodgetts had broken the law, not the banks. Nor did Chifley believe that the Commonwealth Bank could be blamed for what had happened in the Hodgetts case. The matter was an ordinary business transaction into which the Commonwealth Bank would not probe the affairs of either the bank or its client. Chifley had consulted with the Chairman of the Victorian Stock Exchange, which had been conducting audits for the past nine years and he added that Queensland was the only other state to have taken similar action. Chifley suggested that the best way to avoid crimes such as that which Hodgetts had committed was for all stock exchanges to introduce systems to audit their members' accounts.[7]

The Stock Exchange of Adelaide was of a like mind and, as we saw in Chapter 9, it took immediate action to oversee brokers' books and practices before the South Australian Parliament enacted legislation. And well it might. Stock Exchange President Andrew Young said that Hodgetts' failure had caught the Exchange and the rest of Australia by surprise; 'between wind and water'. Indeed, the storm had exposed corrosive barnacles encrusted on the hull of one large ship in the good fleet *Exchange*. Hodgetts had been recognised as a successful broker, a leading light in the Exchange, a prominent figure in sporting and charitable circles, and socially respectable – a solid citizen. Now, he was an embarrassment for the Exchange, which was keen to distance itself from its former secretary, long-serving member and recent committeeman. This proved difficult and, as historian Ron Gibbs put it, 'the story of Hodgetts' demise was doggedly persistent, battering away at the image of the Exchange'.[8] Many Adelaide brokers feared repercussions from Hodgetts' scandal and the press refused to let it lie, given the amount of money involved and public interest. It was bad publicity for the Exchange. Some members lost money. All were unhappy and the vast majority who ran their businesses ethically, prudently and without resort to overdrafts or trading on their own account balked at the heavy criticism levelled at brokers in general.[9]

Fallout for Hodgetts' creditors was long and painful. They raised their concerns from the very beginning when Official Receiver Burns called a meeting on 18 July 1945 in the Boardroom of the Chamber of Manufactures. According to the *Advertiser*, between 70 and 80 people attended. Burns advised creditors that it was difficult to know the true state of Hodgetts' affairs. It would take time. Burns told the meeting that Hodgetts' wife and one of his daughters now claimed his two motorcars, together valued at £500. He assured the meeting that these claims would be investigated. One creditor asked if it were true that the lease on Hodgetts' Cowra Chambers had been transferred to Don

Bradman. Burns advised that this would be revealed in Hodgetts' public examination. Another questioner, representing several clients, asked for a ruling on the position of clients who did not owe money to the bankrupt, but whose scrip Hodgetts had handed to clients from whom he had borrowed. Burns replied that it was likely they would have right of claim of any moneys left over after Hodgetts' debts were paid out.[10]

It was not until 2 December 1948 that Burns announced that a first dividend was to be declared in Hodgetts' estate and that creditors who had not lodged proof of debts by 13 December would be ineligible for a dividend.[11] On 14 January 1949, Burns sought advice in the Bankruptcy Court on a number of issues regarding the distribution of shares and money left over after the pool lender had been paid in full. Judge Paine ruled that where there was a surplus in either cash or shares not sold by the person to whom they had been pledged, owners of shares were entitled to portions of the surplus on a pro rata basis. Main creditor, Guy Fisher, would have at least had some satisfaction when Paine ruled that Hodgetts had no right to pledge his shares to other people.[12]

A second dividend was declared on 9 June 1949.[13] It was to be an even longer process to allocate dividends to creditors and it was another six years after Hodgetts' collapse that Ella Mildred Chomley reclaimed the 570 Broken Hill South shares held in trust for Marion Farr. And, she had to take the Union Bank of South Australia to court to achieve that end.

In a civil sitting before the Chief Justice in July 1953, the bank, the executors of the late Alexander Melrose and late John Andrew Tennant Mortlock, and Mrs Edith Hodgetts were third-party defendants. The bank argued that when Hodgetts pledged the shares in 1944 it had received them in good faith, and that the

Melrose and Mortlock estates and Mrs Hodgetts, as guarantor of her husband's estate, claimed that they were entitled to them as security. The Chief Justice found that Chomley had no reason to think that when she entrusted the shares to Hodgetts he would ever hand them to the bank. He saw no neglect on her part and ordered the return of the shares to Chomley.[14] There were many sad stories. While Fisher was hit hardest – he was a wealthy lawyer who lived at *Pine Hill*, his stately home near Mount Lofty in the Adelaide Hills – there was much sympathy for others, especially for the cricketer Arthur Richardson who lost £8093, his life's savings.[15]

* * *

While the Royal Institute for the Blind was compensated in full, creditor Don Bradman benefited financially from his business mentor's fall, though at some cost to his reputation.

According to Jessie Bradman, when news of Hodgetts' failure broke, 'We were all in shock.' Bradman told author Roland Perry that, 'Despite his folly, we felt sorry for Harry. We believe he was a good man who got caught up in unfortunate circumstances'.[16] In his autobiography, Bradman wrote:

> For me personally there suddenly came a disaster. Overnight the firm by which I was employed went bankrupt. In the midst of a long struggle to regain my health, and through no fault of my own, I became the victim of another's misfortune. There was no time for reflection. I had to make an immediate decision as affecting my whole life. Despite the unprecedented difficulties there were trustworthy friends whose loyalty was responsible for my decision to commence on my own business. I wasn't really fit to carry the strain of the next few months. It would be

idle to try to explain the numerous troubles, which had to be surmounted.[17]

In *Bradman's War: How the 1948 Invincibles Turned the Cricket Pitch into a Battlefield*, Malcolm Knox said that Bradman was referring to how 'quickly he fell on his feet'.[18] For Perry, Bradman turned a setback into an opportunity when he began trading under his own name on the Monday afternoon, two days after Hodgetts had petitioned for bankruptcy.[19] The Exchange Committee and Official Receiver Burns, however, imposed conditions. Bradman had to submit a list of Hodgetts' outstanding settlements, he could not automatically take over the entire clients' list, and he would have to write to as many of these clients as he wished and offer to act as their new broker. Bradman consulted Len Bullock, a broker and another of Hodgetts' former employees. Bullock agreed to join the new venture; and went on to become Bradman's 'right-hand man'.[20]

Writing in 1988, Gibbs explained that Bradman faced the prospect of unemployment and needed to secure his future. As a member of the Exchange Bradman had every right to trade in his own name, but the Exchange's committee accepted his decision to create his own company with remarkably short notice. The decision, and the alacrity with which it was made, aroused curiosity, jealousy and resentment among the public and other brokers. Gibbs suggested that Adelaide's 'small-town, country-town' ways induced gossip and claims that Bradman – and Bullock – must have known of Hodgetts' problems before they became public knowledge.[21] This and the far worse claim that Bradman was involved in Hodgetts' swindle have never been proved. Indeed, Bradman had never been a partner in the business and had no financial interest in it.[22]

But sections of Adelaide's financial establishment disliked that the transfer of the business benefited Bradman immediately, and without due process being followed.[23] Bradman wrote to hundreds of Hodgetts' former clients offering his services. Over time, many former Hodgetts clients invested through Bradman and large commercial institutions and bankers backed him. He developed a reputation as a good broker who offered sound advice. Thus, Bradman's business progressed.[24] Much of this was due to Bullock, Bradman's new right-hand man. Doubtless, the name *Bradman* appealed to clients and companies, as by 1948 the 38-year-old Bradman was a director of five firms as well as being a member of the Stock Exchange.[25] On 1 January 1949, Bradman was knighted for services to cricket. In its report, the *Sydney Morning Herald* said that despite his association with Hodgetts ending in disaster, it had given him a valuable introduction to the Adelaide business world. The paper concluded that, 'Out of the ruins of that first venture, he has built a business of his own, using many of his contacts gained through his cricket career'.[26]

However, Bradman had to ride out some stormy seas. The Hodgetts Affair left its mark on him, and, posthumously, his name. In November 2001, David Nason raised serious issues about Bradman's credibility in two articles published in the *Australian* – 'The Don We Never Knew'. Nason had serious concerns, concerns that some of Bradman's fellow brokers shared. Controversy had erupted when Bradman met with the Exchange Committee and Receiver Burns in secrecy. It usually took a month for the Receiver to decide whether or not a company could trade its way out of trouble and yet here was Bradman allowed to set up business in Hodgetts' fully furnished office 48 hours after his bankruptcy. He was given access to Hodgetts' client list without charge. It was remarkable to allow Hodgetts' former staff access to the 'horribly distorted accounts' when there was the possibility of criminal conduct.

Despite the conditions imposed upon him mentioned above, there was a belief among other brokers that Bradman had assumed ownership of the goodwill of a huge client base. The principle in stockbroking that brokers never approach other brokers' clients was considered inviolable, and as Tom Phillips, Stock Exchange president from 1974 to 1977, put it: 'People accused Bradman of stealing the goodwill of the company and basically they were right.'[27]

Monash University academics Heenan and Dunstan noted the irregularity of handing Bradman the client list and attendant account details instead of auctioning it by tender. Apart from the fact that it was the property of Hodgetts' debtors, auctioning it among other brokers would have improved the chances of clearing some of Hodgetts' debts. Perry refuted these arguments, placing practicality before principle. In his view, the 'goodwill' had been severely damaged and its worth diminished, and there was no point in waiting a month to determine if the company could trade out of trouble as the business was beyond salvaging.[28] Honest and principled brokers were unswayed by that argument and remained convinced that Bradman had received preferential treatment.

Bradman traded under the banner of 'Don Bradman & Company'. The advertising of broking services was frowned upon and on this basis other brokers objected to him using his cricketing name instead of the more formal 'D.G. Bradman' or 'Donald G. Bradman'.[29] In 1946 a press photograph taken of an army sergeant and other 'respectable gentlemen' gathered in front of Bradman's office circulated throughout the country. It showed a sign in the window bearing the words, 'Don Bradman & Co., Stock, Share and Investment Brokers'. Bradman had to front the

Stock Exchange committee, which convened to decide whether or not the photograph amounted to advertising. Bradman denied seeking publicity, adding that he could not control the press and accusing other brokers of concocting a scheme to undermine him. Bradman told Perry, 'It happened because of the jealousies of one or two members, and because of the way the business was progressing.'[30]

Heenan and Dunstan saw Bradman, above all else, as self-serving, a man who exploited his cricketing name for commercial gain. Bradman and Jessie – and Len Bullock – worked hard to build up the business, but the perception prevailed that Bradman had profited from Hodgetts' misfortune. Subsequently, Bradman was ostracised by sections of the 'cliquish Adelaide business establishment': the prestigious Royal Adelaide Golf Club rejected his application for membership. Heenan and Dunstan argue that confronted with hostility from other brokers and the prospect of Hodgetts' creditors pursuing legal proceedings, Bradman returned to cricket, in part to help resurrect the game after World War II and in part to escape scrutiny and social unpleasantness in provincial Adelaide.[31] Indeed, former Stock Exchange president Phillips believed that Bradman became reclusive because he did not wish 'to face hard questioning about the Hodgetts collapse'.[32]

On 29 June 1954, on doctor's orders, Sir Donald Bradman retired from his stockbroking business, but retained an interest in the firm that took over his operation – and its goodwill – Len Bullock & Co. Bradman retained his place as South Australian Delegate to the Australian Cricket Board of Control, a position he had taken over from none other than Henry Warburton Hodgetts Jnr in 1945 and while still a player.[33]

* * *

Yatala Labour Prison, c. 1974. Hodgetts served his sentence in the buildings seen behind the modern wall and tower.
(Photo: John Healey. Courtesy State Library of South Australia, B 76329)

On being sentenced, Hodgetts was incarcerated in Yatala Labour Prison. Located in Northfield, the prison was built in 1854 so that prisoners could quarry rock from nearby Dry Creek for much-needed road and construction works. In 1945 some original buildings still existed, but prisoners no longer broke rocks. Former broker Hodgetts could try his hand at a trade: he could choose from boot making, tin smithing, blacksmithing, carpentry and masonry.[34] His experience in gaol has not been documented, but he was an ill man who must have found his imprisonment doubly difficult.

We know that Edith Hodgetts visited her husband, and on occasions the headmistress of Girton, Dorothy Yates, accompanied her. As mentioned, Girton publicly distanced itself from its former Board chairman, but Yates was a devout Christian, of whom it was said, 'she hated the sin, but loved the sinner'. Yates gave Edith Hodgetts her unqualified support in what was for her a very difficult time.[35]

It is likely that other members of his family and some friends visited him in gaol. In January 1947 Hodgetts received two surprise visitors, Chief Inspector Wilfred 'Flappy' Daws and Detective Sergeant Ernest Miller of Scotland Yard. Daws and Miller had arrived in Australia in 1946 to investigate an alleged £8,000,000 mining fraud in Western Australia. They were based in Melbourne at the Russell Street headquarters of Victoria Police and in the course of their investigations visited Adelaide and Kalgoorlie. They visited Hodgetts in the hope that he could provide information about the alleged fraud.[36] Nothing more was heard of this visit or the outcome of the detectives' inquiries, other than the fact 'Flappy' Daws married Roberta Grant, the Russell Street typist assigned to assist him. The happy couple lived at Clapham Common, London, while Hodgetts languished in Yatala.[37]

The press reported that Hodgetts spent several periods in hospital during his gaol term. What Gibbs called the 'racier publications' had referred to Hodgetts as the 'former debonair man-about-town' and the 'well-dressed Grenfell Street commercial business leviathan'.[38] True to form, on Sunday 3 August 1947, the Sydney *Truth* announced that Hodgetts was dangerously ill in the Royal Adelaide Hospital, declaring that the 'Broker-Gambler Is Now In Death's Shadow, Swindler May Die'.[39] Despite the *Truth* claiming that the authorities might remit the balance of Hodgetts' sentence and discharge him from legal custody when he was released from hospital, and the *Canberra Times* declaring in July 1948 that Hodgetts was to be released, he survived in gaol for another year before he was again transferred to hospital where he died.

Hodgetts was buried privately at St George's Cemetery, Magill, on Wednesday 5 October 1949, aged 67.[40] Death did not save his name from infamy. When *Truth* ran a series of articles in 1952 under the headline 'Rogues of the Stock Exchange', it devoted Number 1 to Henry Warburton Hodgetts Jnr.[41]

'Rogues of the Stock Exchange' (*Truth*, 24 August 1952, p. 14)

Epilogue

Author Roland Perry described Hodgetts' fall from grace as being 'of Mayor of Casterbridge proportion'.[1] Indeed, there are several similarities between Thomas Hardy's protagonist, Michael Henchard, and Harry Hodgetts. Both started with little, prospered and gained respect, only to lose everything through their own doing and some bad luck. Henchard and Hodgetts self-destructed. Both made risky business decisions that led to disaster, resulting in their employees taking over their businesses. Henchard spent his final years alone and Hodgetts was incarcerated in prison.

In his contribution to *The New Cambridge Companion To Shakespeare*, Michael Neill explained that Shakespearean tragedies, above all, deal with the downfall of the mighty.[2] Was Hodgetts mighty? He was one of Adelaide's successful and highly respected businessmen, a generous supporter of educational and sporting institutions, and a debonair, sociable man who entertained in style. Adelaideans recognised him. Indeed, he was a man who stood out in a crowd, be it in the city, at formal occasions, gatherings of the elite or at the Adelaide Oval. He may not have been particularly noteworthy outside his hometown,

Epilogue

but in provincial Adelaide his self-induced downfall was tragic.

Stuart Macintyre noted that class-based history of Australia reached its high-water mark in the 1980s. Since then, the tide has been out, despite material inequality remaining deeply entrenched in Australia. The language of class and class-consciousness – 'upper', 'middle' and 'working' classes for example – has been replaced with terms such as 'true believers' and 'the battlers' for workers, and 'the forgotten people' and 'middle Australia' for the middle classes.[3] Where historians and sociologists had once written in terms of class, power and status – they are related, but different – it is common now to hear references to 'the political class', a marrying of class and power that illustrates a lack of understanding of those terms, where class is essentially determined by a person's role in the economic system and power relates to the ability, or lack of it, to influence the political, legal and coercive instruments of authority. Although class-based history is not currently fashionable, material inequalities exist. While some people have high status, others have greater ability to influence governments in their decision-making. And so it was in Hodgetts' day.

In the context of mid-20th century Adelaide, Hodgetts was an upper-class man of high standing. He showed little interest in politics, and only became an active lobbyist in the final and failing years of his career. He was well known, obviously wealthy and influential in sports administration – with, perhaps, his eye on the possibility of a future knighthood – but in terms of political power he was far from mighty. Hodgetts' public humiliation was tragic, but it lacked the gravitas of Shakespearean tragedies, which dealt with the rise and fall of the truly mighty – absolute monarchs. Perry's claim that it was 'of Mayor of Casterbridge proportions' was closer to the mark and has merit.

In 1958, British sociologist Michael Young published *The Rise of the Meritocracy*, in which he argued that intelligence and merit would replace the old class-based distinctions as the key factors that shape society. A highly educated, able elite would rise to the pinnacle of power.[4] In the future, intelligence, education and effort, rather than wealth and family background, would be to the fore. It was well for Hodgetts that he was a self-made man in the first half of the 20th century when it was more common to reach the highest ranks of society on grit and graft alone. We must not, however, underestimate his business acumen that underpinned his initial success. Possibly his wife's family background bore heavily on him. He was ambitious, optimistic and acquisitive and he set out to provide the very best lifestyle he could for his family.

That he achieved, but his business was built upon an unstable foundation. He relied heavily on borrowed money and bank overdrafts. And there were questions about the very probity of trading on the stock market. Floating a public company to raise capital is sound business practice, so long as the value of the company keeps pace with the value of its shares. Raising money for a company is not always commensurate with the interests of investors who demand a good return on their money. When former Australian Treasurer, Peter Costello, encouraged 'mum and dad investors' to try their hand in the market they often found themselves at the mercy of cashed-up national and foreign investment companies, very big bears and bulls, not to mention wildcats. Investing on the stock market is risky.

Hodgetts was in a risky business that also fostered speculation. Sections of the various churches had long railed against gambling at the racecourse and at the Stock Exchange. And at church fairs! That, however, did not prevent some clergymen from investing on the stock market, and his fellow

Epilogue

Methodist ministers reprimanded the Rev. B.G. Edwards when he was charged over a breach of share contract in 1888. The Church demanded that Edwards 'desist such pursuits in the future' and its denouncements of share trading pressured him into resigning.[5] Hodgetts gambled and lost when he speculated in wheat futures. Seemingly a less risky venture, his involvement in the Darwin Hotel syndicate proved disastrous.

When his Broken Hill agent, Allan Hall, defaulted and suicided, Hodgetts suffered a substantial setback and was left to pay John Gorman £1740 and his legal costs in 1932. It was evident that Hall had both speculated in mining and cashed in clients' shares to pay other clients. The lesson was there for Hodgetts. Yet when he knew in 1940 that he was in financial trouble he embarked upon a path similar to the one that Hall had trod. Hodgetts knew it was wrong, despite his claim that it was common practice among brokers to rob Peter to pay Paul, and to pay back Peter when funds were available, with no one knowing. Illegal and risky business, indeed! We can, perhaps, excuse the syndicate to which Hodgetts belonged for investing so heavily in Darwin hotels in 1940, as this investment was made nearly two years before the Japanese attacked Pearl Harbor and, shortly after, Darwin itself. Yet, earlier, in November 1938, Port Kembla wharf labourers had refused to load pig iron bound for the Japan Steel Works, which made bombs used in expansionist Japan's invasion of China.[6] A forward-looking syndicate might have thought twice about investing in Darwin. Things went awry for Hodgetts and he was unfortunate that World War II and the trading restrictions consequently imposed dragged on and his major backer, Alexander Melrose, died in September 1944, about nine months before his downfall.

His Counsel, J.W. Nelligan, primarily blamed Hodgetts' failure on his optimistic approach to trading. Hodgetts knew in 1940 that he was on dangerous ground and chose to pursue an unethical, illegal path to trade his way out of trouble when he was hopelessly in debt. Perhaps it was more the action of a desperate and proud man who feared the shame associated with the public disclosure of his failed business. He had little more than hope. What Hodgetts did was criminal. He hurt many clients and damaged the reputation of other brokers and the Stock Exchange. He presented a tragic figure at his trial. Unlike Hall, however, Hodgetts had the courage to face judgment, pleaded guilty and saved the public purse the expense of a protracted trial.

In *The Mayor of Casterbridge*, Michael Henchard's employee took over his business, just as Bradman superseded Hodgetts, his business mentor. Bradman also replaced Hodgetts as the South Australian delegate to the Australian Board of Cricket Control. Bradman was knighted. Hodgetts languished in gaol. Hodgetts' tragedy was complete.

* * *

It is useful to add a brief historiographical note in respect of the discussion about class, power and influence. So-called 'old left' historians such as Russell Ward displayed an optimistic assessment of the role of the labour movement in shaping Australia. By contrast 'new left' historians such as Humphrey McQueen presented a more pessimistic account of its role. Similarly, those biographers who wrote before Sir Donald Bradman's death generally penned favourable accounts and focused mainly on his cricket career, while later analysts searched more deeply and widely and cast a more critical eye over 'The Don's' personal life and his business affairs.

Notes

Introduction

1. Mrs Lillie Smith operated Girton House, Girls' Grammar School in Kent Town from 1915 until ill health forced her to step down at the end of 1925. A group of parents bought and ran it as an independent, corporate school – Girton Proprietary School for Girls. The Kent Town property sufficed for 1926, but in 1927 the school moved to 18 Holden Street, Kensington Park, the former residence of James Alexander Holden. See John Davis, 2014, *Principles & Pragmatism: Vol. 1* for a detailed history of Girton.
2. Case of H.W. Hodgetts (September 13, 1945). *Chronicle*, p. 25. Retrieved November 3, 2021, from http://nla.gov.au/nla.news-article93340082.
3. Hodgetts Gets 5 Years (September 10, 1945). *News*, p. 1. Retrieved October 27, 2021, from http://nla.gov.au/nla.news-article11118916.

Chapter 1 – The Making of Harry and Edith Hodgetts

1. See Approaching Marriages (September 28, 1912). *Chronicle*, p. 56. Retrieved December 2, 2021, from http://nla.gov.au/nla.news-page8735687, and Marriages – Hodgetts – Gwynne (November 14, 1912). *Register*, p. 8. Retrieved November 18, 2021, from http://nla.gov.au/nla.news-page4509742. Hodgetts and his wife both adopted given names different from those on their birth certificates to avoid confusion with Harry's father and Mary's mother respectively, with whom they each shared their first given names, and second in Harry's case. In the formal announcement of their engagement in the *Register*, 14 November 1912, their birth-certificate names were used, but the social page of the *Chronicle*, 28 November 1912, refers to the approaching marriage of 'Miss Edith Gwynne and Mr H. Hodgetts'. In 1945 'H.W. Hodgetts (trust account E. Hodgetts)' is listed among

Hodgetts' creditors. 'E. Hodgetts' undoubtedly referred to Edith. See Hodgetts' Estate Creditors Listed (July 7, 1945). *News*, p. 1. Retrieved June 4, 2022, from http://nla.gov.au/nla.news-article130234725 and Deficiency of $82,854 (July 11, 1945). *Weekly Times*, p. 4. Retrieved October 28, 2021, from http://nla.gov.au/nla.news-article226558760. Newspaper reports of events at which Edith attended without her husband referred to her as 'Mrs H.W. Hodgetts', as was then the norm.

2   See *Sands & McDougall's South Australian Directory For 1912*, 1912, Sands and McDougall, Adelaide, pp. 799 & 1165. The 1912 Directory lists Harry Hodgetts as the secretary of the Stock Exchange of Adelaide, but does not give a private residential address for him. It shows his father and mother as living at Tea Tree Gully, and his mother as the postmistress. His father had become blind and could no longer carry out his post office duties. The newspaper wedding notices described Harry as living at Tea Tree Gully and it is almost certain that he was then living with his parents.

3   See Hodgetts – Gwynne Wedding (October 26, 1912). *Chronicle*, p. 56. Retrieved December 2, 2021, from http://nla.gov.au/nla.news-page8735943.

4   Peter F. McDonald, *Age at First Marriage and Proportions Marrying in Australia 1860–1971*, Thesis, Australian National University, 1972, p. 183. McDonald showed that the median age for marriage in Australia in 1911 was 26.8 years for men and 23.8 years for women.

5   See David St Leger Kelly, 'Gwynne, Edward Castres (1811–1888)', *Australian Dictionary of Biography*, National Centre of Biography, Australian National University, https://adb.edu.au/biography/gwynne-edward-castres-368/text5759, accessed online 25 November 2021, and Dirk van Dissel, *The Adelaide Gentry, 1850–1920*, in Richards, Eric, (ed.), 1986, *The Flinders History of South Australia, Social History*, Wakefield Press, Netley, p. 344.

6   H. Kempe, 'Mortlock, William Ransom (1821–1884)', *Australian Dictionary of Biography*, National Centre of Biography, Australian University, https://adb.edu.au/biography/mortlock-william-ransom-4259/text6839, accessed online 24 November 2021, Dirk van Dissel, *The Adelaide Gentry, 1850–1920*, op. cit., p. 347, Family Notices (1877, September 26). *Express and Telegraph*, p. 2 (2nd edn). Retrieved November 18, 2021, from http://nla.gov.au/nla.news-article20757642 and *Redlegs Museum, History of the Norwood Football Club* at http://www.redlegsmuseum.com.au/ON_FIELD/PLAYERS/GWYNNEEdward.aspxhttp://www.redlegsmuseum.com.au/ON_FIELD/PLAYERS/GWYNNEEdward.aspx

Notes

7 Mariah Long, Senior Archives officer, Special Collections, Barr Smith Library, University of Adelaide provided information about Edward Gwynne's university studies.
8 John Davis, 2014, *Principles & Pragmatism: Vol. 1 A History of Girton and King's College, the antecedents of Pembroke School*, Wakefield Press, Adelaide, p. 9.
9 Local Art Examination (1894, December 11). *Express and Telegraph*, p. 3 (2nd edn). Retrieved November 18, 2021, from http://nla.gov.au/nla.news-article209045095; and Local Art and Science Examinations (1895, December 16). *South Australian Register*, p. 6. Retrieved November 18, 2021, from http://nla.gov.au/nla.news-article53663471.
10 *The Unitarian Annie Montgomerie Martin educates brilliant girls vital to suffrage push in South Australia* at https://adelaideaz.com/articles/unitarian-schoolteacher-annie-montgomerie-martin-educates-brilliant-girls-crucial-to-suffrage-future.
11 Davis, op. cit., p. 5. Lillie Thompson married James Smith, an Adelaide stockbroker, and when the Stock Exchange closed for seven weeks in August and September 1914, as Lillie Smith, she made arrangements to open Girton House Girls' Grammar School in 1915. It was one of her most able students who used the term 'clever ladies'.
12 *Australian Home Beautiful*, Vol. 11 No. 5, 1 May 1933, pp. 19–21.
13 Obituary (July 4, 1944). *Advertiser*, p. 7. Retrieved November 4, 2021, from http://nla.gov.au/nla.news-article43210887 and *Private Sources at the National Archives, Private Accessions 1997–2002,* National Archives of Ireland at https://www.nationalarchives.ie/wp-content/uploads/2019/03/PrivateAccessions1997-2002.pdf.
14 Jan Thomas (ed.), 1997, *South Australian Births Index of Registration 1842 to 1906*, Vol. 4 H, South Australian Genealogy & Heraldry Society Inc., South Australia, p. 1363.
15 *Sands & McDougall's South Australian Directory For 1899*, 1899, Sands and McDougall, Adelaide, p. 546.
16 See State Library of South Australia at https://collections.slsa.sa.gov.au/resource/B+8106.
17 Old College School. (1897, December 18). *Advertiser*, p. 5. Retrieved October 28, 2021, from http://nla.gov.au/nla.news-article35100137.
18 St Peter's College School Archivist Andrea McKinnon-Matthews provided this information. In 1898, schools used a four-term year.
19 R.M. Gibbs, 'Hodgetts, Henry Warburton (Harry) (1882–1949)', *Australian Dictionary of Biography*, National Centre of Biography, Australian University, https://adb.anu.edu.au/biography/hodgetts-henry-warburton-harry-10514/text18659, accessed online 28 October

2012, Honoured Sportsman (May 5, 1923). *Observer*, p. 51. Retrieved September 1, 2022, from http://nla.gov.au/nla.news-article164823559 and *Who's Who: South Australia Centenary, 1936*: p. 198.
20 David St Leger Kelly, op. cit.

Chapter 2 – Making Good

1 See Graeme Davison's contribution to *The Oxford Companion To Australian History*. Graeme Davison, John Hurst & Stuart Macintyre, 1998, *The Oxford Companion To Australian History*, Oxford University Press, Melbourne, p. 521.
2 See R.M. Gibbs, 1988, *Bulls, Bears and Wildcats: A Centenary History of the Stock Exchange of Adelaide*, Peacock Publications, Norwood, p. 213, and Average Wages. (June 8, 1914). *Sydney Morning Herald*, p. 9. Retrieved September 1, 2022, from http://nla.gov.au/nla.news-article15514184. Hodgetts' salary is an estimation based on available evidence. In 1920, 10 years after Hodgetts became secretary, the Exchange increased Secretary C.A.M. West's annual income from ₤250 to ₤300 and increased Caller H.M. Good's income to ₤270. The details regarding average wages were taken from the *Sydney Morning Herald* article.
3 Gibbs, op. cit., pp. 97, 100 and 140–143.
4 Gibbs, op. cit., p. 182.
5 Gibbs, op. cit., pp. 101 and 139–140.
6 Gibbs, op. cit., p. 141.
7 Gibbs, op. cit., p. 211.
8 Stock Exchange Rifle Club (March 2, 1915). *Express and Telegraph*, p. 1 (special war edition). Retrieved November 8, 2021, from http://nla.gov.au/nla.news-article209971460.
9 Gibbs, op. cit., p. 199.
10 R.M. Gibbs, op. cit., p. 144.
11 See Gibbs, op. cit., pp. 143–152 for a detailed description of brokers' lifestyles and interests.
12 Gibbs, op. cit., p. 211.
13 See *Sands & McDougall's South Australian Directories*, Sands and McDougall, Adelaide, 1913, p. 876; 1920, p. 1084 and 1927, p. 1212. Current owners of Carlshurst, Andrea and David Crase, have extracts from the Department of the Registrar General showing the transfer of ownership of land from Charlotte Reinecke to Henry Warburton Hodgetts Jnr, on 3 December 1918. *Sands & McDougall's South Australian Directories* place Hodgetts at 3 Walsall Street, Kensington Park, from 1913 to 1919, at 36 Park Road from 1920 to 1926, and at 40

Park Road from 1927. The 1918 extract from the Registrar General cites his address as 'Walsall Street'. Hodgetts bought the property in 1918 and, perhaps, allowed Charlotte, wife of recently deceased Charles (Carl) Reinecke, to continue living there.

14 Elizabeth Warburton, 1981, *The Paddocks Beneath, A History of Burnside from the Beginning*, Corporation of the City of Burnside, Adelaide, p. 246, *SA Heritage Places Database Search*, at https://maps.sa.gov.au/heritagesearch/Heritageitem.aspx?p_heritageno=8206 and Angela Steinberner, Burnside Historical Survey cited online at https://data.environment.sa.gov.au/Content/heritage-surveys/3-Burnside-Heritage-Survey-Part-3-B-Items-O-Y-1987.pdf.

15 Elizabeth Warburton, op. cit., p. 296. *Sands & McDougall's South Australian Directory For 1944–45*, p. 942 records C.W.L. Hodgetts' address as 133 Grant Avenue, Toorak Gardens.

16 Hodgetts Case Creditors Meet (July 19, 1945). *Advertiser*, p. 3. Retrieved November 3, 2021, from http://nla.gov.au/nla.news-article43502659.

17 St Peter's College School Archivist, Andrea McKinnon-Matthews, provided this information.

18 Pembroke School Archivist, Peta Harries, provided this information.

19 John Davis, 2014, *Principles & Pragmatism: Vol. 1 A History of Girton and King's College, the antecedents of Pembroke School*, Wakefield Press, Adelaide, pp. 40–41 and 50–51.

20 Gibbs, op. cit., p. 304.

21 Bankruptcy: Hodgetts Case In Third Day (August 9, 1945). *Advertiser*, p. 7. Retrieved November 3, 2021, from http://nla.gov.au/nla.news-article43505836.

22 Supreme Court: Woman Recovers Shares (July 2,1 1951). *Advertiser*, p. 4. Retrieved October 28, 2021, from http://nla.gov.au/nla.news-article45719757.

23 R.M. Gibbs, 'Hodgetts, Henry Warburton (Harry) (1882–1949)', *Australian Dictionary of Biography*, National Centre of Biography, Australian University, https://adb.anu.edu.au/biography/hodgetts-henry-warburton-harry-10514/text18659, accessed online 28 October 2012 and Arrested Man At Court (July 14, 1945). *News*, p. 1. Retrieved October 28, 2021, from http://nla.gov.au/nla.news-article130327589.

24 Rogues of the Stock Exchange (August 24, 1952). *Truth*, p. 14. Retrieved November 3, 2021, from http://nla.gov.au/nla.news-article168007621.

25 ibid. and Gibbs, op. cit., p. 302.

26 Brokers To Pay £1,740 (December 16, 1932). *News*, p. 7. Retrieved August 10, 2022, from http://nla.gov.au/nla.news-article128939649, Supreme Court: Woman Recovers Shares (July 21, 1951). *Advertiser*, p. 4. Retrieved October 28, 2021, from http://nla.gov.au/nla.news-article45719757, Bankruptcy: Hodgetts Case In Third Day (August 9, 1945). *Advertiser*, p. 7. Retrieved November 3, 2021, from http://nla.gov.au/nla.news-article43505836 and Case of H.W. Hodgetts: Five Years' Gaol (September 13, 1945). *Chronicle*, p. 25. Retrieved November 3, 2021, from http://nla.gov.au/nla.news-article93340082.

27 No Privilege of Silence (August 7, 1945). *Newcastle Morning Herald and Miners' Advocate*, p. 3. Retrieved October 28, 2021, from http://nla.gov.au/nla.news-article134357148.

28 Gibbs, op. cit., p. 233.

29 Davis, op. cit., p. 82.

30 See Gibbs, op. cit., pp. 233–250 for a detailed discussion of the Depression's effect on brokers, companies, governments and stock exchanges.

31 Michael Kitson, *End of an Epoch: Britain's Withdrawal from the Gold Standard*, Judge Business School, University of Cambridge, June 2012 at https://michaelkitson.files.wordpress.com/2013/02/kitson-gold-standard-june-2021.pdf.

32 Gibbs, op. cit., pp. 252–253.

33 Romantic Story of Revival on Change (December 10, 1932). *Mail*, p. 8. Retrieved November 4, 2021, from http://nla.gov.au/nla.news-article59832992.

34 Gibbs, op. cit., p. 258.

35 Gibbs, op. cit., p. 270.

36 Mining News: W.A. Goldmining Industry: Adelaide Broker's Impressions of Tour (June 19, 1936). *Advertiser*, p. 21. Retrieved November 9, 2021, from http://nla.gov.au/nla.news-article48154774.

37 *Who's Who: South Australia Centenary, 1936*, The Amalgamated Publishing Company, Adelaide, 1 September 1936, p. 198.

38 See Progress at Darwin (January 4, 1940). *Chronicle*, p. 58. Retrieved November 3, 2021, from http://nla.gov.au/nla.news-page8693883.

39 *Who's Who*, op. cit., p. 204.

Chapter 3 – A Good Sport, An Outstanding Sports Administrator

1 Prominent Sportsman (September 22, 1923). *News*, p. 5 (home edition). Retrieved October 28, 2021, from http://nla.gov.au/nla.news-article129847074.

Notes

2 Honoured Sportsman (May 5, 1923). *Observer*, p. 51. Retrieved November 3, 2021, from http://nla.gov.au/nla.news-article164823559.
3 H.W. Hodgetts (August 26 ,1910). *Express and Telegraph*, p. 6 (4 o'clock edition sports number). Retrieved November 3, 2021, from http://nla.gov.au/nla.news-article209909137; and Prominent Sportsman (September 22, 1923). *News*, p. 5 (home edition). Retrieved October 28, 2021, from http://nla.gov.au/nla.news-article129847074.
4 Mr H.W. Hodgetts (September 27, 1928). *News*, p. 15 (home edition). Retrieved November 3, 2021, from http://nla.gov.au/nla.news-article129170109.
5 See Cricket: Matches Today (February 15, 1919). *Advertiser*, p. 7. Retrieved November 3, 2021, from http://nla.gov.au/nla.news-page987030.
6 'Old Boys' Day' At S.P.C.A. (sic) (December 5, 1925). *Mail*, p. 5. Retrieved November 3, 2021, from http://nla.gov.au/nla.news-article59961986.
7 A New Golf Language Introduced By Cricket Legislator (April 30, 1936). *Referee (Sydney, NSW: 1886–1939)*, p. 2. Retrieved November 3, 2021, from http://nla.gov.au/nla.news-article13560721.
8 See Continuous Cricket (November 29, 1934). *Chronicle*, p. 66. Retrieved November 3, 2021, from http://nla.gov.au/nla.news-page8671908.
9 Lad of 43 (April 27, 1936). *Sun*, p. 11 (country edition). Retrieved November 3, 2021, from http://nla.gov.au/nla.news-article230821372.
10 Honoured Sportsman (May 5, 1923). *Observer*, p. 51. Retrieved November 3, 2021, from http://nla.gov.au/nla.news-article164823559.
11 Rifle Shooting (March 2, 1916). *Register*, p. 9. Retrieved November 8, 2021, from http://nla.gov.au/nla.news-article59630592.
12 ibid.
13 Mr. H.W. Hodgetts (September 27, 1928). *News*, p. 15 (home edition). Retrieved November 3, 2021, from http://nla.gov.au/nla.news-article129170109.
14 People in Sport (July 31, 1925). *News*, p. 8 (home edition). Retrieved November 3, 2021, from http://nla.gov.au/nla.news-article129791361.
15 Honoured Sportsman (May 5, 1923). *Observer*, p. 51. Retrieved November 3, 2021, from http://nla.gov.au/nla.news-article164823559; and Mr. H.W. Hodgetts (September 2,7 1928). *News*, p. 15 (home edition). Retrieved November 3, 2021, from http://nla.gov.au/nla.news-article129170109.
16 Personal (July 11, 1923). *Register*, p. 8. Retrieved November 3, 2021, from http://nla.gov.au/nla.news-article643095525.

17 *Paris or the Bush doco about 1924 Olympic Rowing team The Cods premieres in Murray Bridge* (April 23, 2016). ABC news documentary.
18 Mr. H.W. Hodgetts (September 27, 1928). *News*, p. 15 (home edition). Retrieved November 3, 2021, from http://nla.gov.au/nla.news-article129170109.
19 Prominent Sportsman (September 22, 1923). *News*, p. 5 (home edition). Retrieved November 3, 2021, from http://nla.gov.au/nla.news-article129847074; Lacrosse President For 14 Years (March 12, 1934). *News*, p. 9. Retrieved November 3, 2021, from http://nla.gov.au/nla.news-article128855592; and *Who's Who: South Australia Centenary, 1936*, The Amalgamated Publishing Company, Adelaide, 1 September 1936, p. 198.
20 Lacrosse (May 9, 1908). *Evening Journal (Adelaide, SA: 1869–1912)*, p. 8 (late edition). Retrieved November 3, 2021, from http://nla.gov.au/nla.news-article208630074. Smoke socials were exclusively male social events held in Australia in the late 19th and early 20th centuries.
21 Lacrosse (July 23, 1910). *West Australian*, p. 13. Retrieved February 2, 2022, from http://nla.gov.au/nla.news-article26263583.
22 Lacrosse in Egypt (March 27, 1915). *Mail*, p. 5. Retrieved November 3, 2021, from http://nla.gov.au/nla.news-article59301731.
23 Mr. H.W. Hodgetts (September 27, 1928). *News*, p. 15 (home edition). Retrieved November 3, 2021, from http://nla.gov.au/nla.news-article129170109; and *Adelaide East Herald*, 3 February 2022, p. 11. In 1921, the East Torrens District Cricket Club awarded life membership to Hodgetts in appreciation of his service to the club.
24 ibid. and *Who's Who: South Australia Centenary, 1936*, op. cit., p. 198.
25 Honoured Sportsman (May 5, 1923). *Observer*, p. 51. Retrieved November 3, 2021, from http://nla.gov.au/nla.news-article164823559; and Mr. H.W. Hodgetts (September 27, 1928). *News*, p. 15 (home edition). Retrieved November 3, 2021, from http://nla.gov.au/nla.news-article129170109.
26 South Australian Visitor (May 25, 1936). *West Australian*, p. 14. Retrieved November 3, 2021, from http://nla.gov.au/nla.news-article40718968.
27 The Sportsman (September 19, 1931). *Australasian*, p. 48. Retrieved August 30, 2022, from http://nla.gov.au/nla.news-article140840964.
28 The Bodyline cables/ Australian Board sends the infamous protest message to MCC at https://www.cricketcountry.com/articles/the-bodyline-cables-australian-board-sends-the-infamous-protest-message-to-mcc-86804.

Notes

29 David Frith, 2002, *Bodyline Autopsy: The Full Story of the most sensational Test Cricket series: Australia v England 1932–1933*, ABC Books, Sydney. Accessed online at https://books.google.com.au/books/about/Bodyline_Autopsy.html?id=zvQ1AAAACAAJ&redir_esc=y'

30 Mr H. Hodgetts Likely Cricket Board Chairman (August 19, 1939). *Telegraph (Brisbane, Qld.: 1872–1947)*, p. 7. Retrieved November 3, 2021, from http://nla.gov.au/nla.news-article184891587.

31 Cited in *Cricket Australia: Our History* at https://www.cricketaustralia.com.au/about/our-history.

Chapter 4 – Brokering a Deal with Bradman

1 Roland Perry, 2021, *Bradman Vs Bodyline: The inside story of the most notorious Ashes series in history*, Allen & Unwin, Crows Nest, p. 287.

2 Bradman's New Position (February 24, 1934). *Avon Argus and Cunderdin-Meckering-Tammin Mail*, p. 6. Retrieved November 3, 2021, from http://nla.gov.au/nla.news-article251919918; Don Bradman (February 23, 1934). *Daily Mercury*, p. 9. Retrieved November 3, 2021, from http://nla.gov.au/nla.news-article172784143; and Bradman Moving. Hodgetts Confirms Story (February 15, 1934). *Daily Standard (Brisbane, Qld.: 1912–1936)*, p. 6 (first edition). Retrieved October 28, 2021, from http://nla.gov.au/nla.news-article186784730.

3 Don Bradman (February 15, 1934). *Sydney Morning Herald*, p. 11. Retrieved January 28, 2022, from http://nla.gov.au/nla.news-article170483347.

4 John A. Daly, 'Grimmett, Clarence Victor (Clarrie) (1891–1980), *Australian Dictionary of Biography*, National Centre of Biography, Australian National University, https:adb.anu.au/biography/grimmett-clarence-vistor-clarrie-6493/text11133, accessed online on 24 February 2022; and Cricket (April 14, 1927). *Sport*, p. 8. Retrieved September 1, 2022, from http://nla.gov.au/nla.news-article215973903. Travers and McCarron had arranged for Grimmett to play for the Adelaide District Cricket Club. They organised accommodation and a testimonial for him, but were displeased when he changed residence and played for the Kensington Club.

5 Don Bradman (February 13, 1934). *Sydney Morning Herald*, p. 9. Retrieved January 28, 2022, from http://nla.gov.au/nla.news-article17047592. Clayvel Lindsay ('Jack') Badcock (1914–1982) represented Australia in seven test matches between 1936 and 1938.

6 Don Bradman (February 15, 1934). *Chronicle*, p. 41. Retrieved November 3, 2021, from http://nla.gov.au/nla.news-article92357541.

7   Tom Heenan and David Dunstan, *Don Bradman: Just a boy from Bowral* in Bateman, Anthony & Hill, Jeffrey, (eds), 2011, *The Cambridge Companion to Cricket*, Cambridge University Press, Cambridge, pp. 94–95.
8   Roland Perry, 2019, *Tea and Scotch with Bradman*, HarperCollins Publishers, Australia Pty Limited for ABC Books, Sydney, p. 128.
9   Roland Perry, From batting to broking, in *Financial Review*, 25 October 1996 cited at https://www.afr.com/politics/from-batting-to-broking-19961025-k75bi.
10 Bradman Here On March 10 (February 15, 1934). *Advertiser*, p. 9. Retrieved October 28, 2021, from http://nla.gov.au/nla.news-article47536683; and Don Bradman Has Played His Last Game With N.S.W. (February 14, 1934). *Newcastle Sun (NSW: 1918–1954)*, p. 7. Retrieved November 3, 2021, from http://nla.gov.au/nla.news-article166247069.
11 Roland Perry, From batting to broking, in *Financial Review*, op. cit.
12 ibid.
13 Roland Perry, 2019, *Tea and Scotch with Bradman*, op. cit., p. 125.
14 Michael Page, *The Bradman Collection*, The State Library of South Australia at https://www.slsa.sa.gov.au/bradmans-biography.
15 *Controversies involving Don Bradman*, at https://en.wikipedia.org/wiki/Controversies_involving_Don_Bradman.
16 Accrington Cricket Club web site at *Accringtoncc.com*.
17 Bradman and Adelaide (February 14, 1934). *Australian Worker*, p. 12. Retrieved January 28, 2022, from http://nla.gov.au/nla.news-article146163848.
18 Roland Perry, 2021, *Bradman Vs Bodyline: The inside story of the most notorious Ashes series in history*, op. cit.
19 Bradman Travels Incognito (March 14, 1934). *West Australian*, p. 16. Retrieved November 3, 2021, from http://nla.gov.au/nla.news-article32991534.
20 David Dunstan and Tom Heenan, 2014, *Shattering the Myth*, Monash University at https://www.monash.edu/news/opinions/shattering-the-myth.
21 For a detailed account of Heenan and Dunstan's thesis see Tom Heenan and David Dunstan, *Don Bradman: Just a boy from Bowral*, op. cit., pp. 94–95; David Dunstan and Tom Heenan, 2014, *Shattering the Myth*, Monash University at https://www.monash.edu/news/opinions/shattering-the-myth; and Thomas Frank Heenan & William David Dunstan, 2015, *A man on the make: the business of being

Bradman, Monash University at https://research.monash.edu/en/publications/a-man-on-the-make-the-business-of-being-bradman.
22 Bradman For Adelaide. (February 2,1 1934). *Australian Worker*, p. 12. Retrieved August 30, 2022, from http://nla.gov.au/nla.news-article146162762.
23 Bradman Travels Incognito (March 14, 1934). *West Australian*, p. 16. Retrieved November 3, 2021, from http://nla.gov.au/nla.news-article32991534, p. 16; and Bradman Here On March 10 (February 15, 1934). *Advertiser*, p. 9. Retrieved October 28, 2021, from http://nla.gov.au/nla.news-article475366683.
24 Bradman Moving To Adelaide (February 16, 1934). *Scone Advocate*, p. 5. Retrieved January 28, 2022, from http://nla.gov.au/nla.news-article158064585; Don Bradman (February 15 1934). *Examiner*, p. 7 (daily). Retrieved November 3, 2021, from http://nla.gov.au/nla.news-article51857186; Bradman For S.A. (February 21, 1934). *Manning River Times and Advocate for the Northern Coast Districts of New South Wales*, p. 3. Retrieved November 3, 2021, from http://nla.gov.au/nla.news-article171832945; and Bradman's New Position (February 1934 24). *Avon Argus and Cunderdin-Meckering-Tammin Mail*, p. 6. Retrieved November 3, 2021, from http://nla.gov.au/nla.news-article251919918.
25 Bradman Here on March 10 (February 15, 1934). *Advertiser*, p. 9. Retrieved October 28, 2021, from http://nla.gov.au/nla.news-article47536683. See Angela Steinberner, Burnside Historical Survey cited online at https://data.environment.sa.gov.au/Content/heritage-surveys/3-Burnside-Heritage-Survey-Part-3-B-Items-O-Y-1987.pdf. James Gosse lived at 40 Park Road Kensington Park at some time after Hodgetts. According to current owners, Andrea and David Crase, Gosse once claimed that Don and Jessie Bradman had lived with Hodgetts while their house at 2 Holden Street was being built.
26 Don Bradman (February 23, 1934). *Daily Mercury*, p. 9. Retrieved November 3, 2021, from http://nla.gov.au/nla.news-article172784143.
27 Bundle of Letters. To Young Cricketers (February 16, 1934). *Sun*, p. 11 (final extra). Retrieved January 28, 2022, from http://nla.gov.au/nla.news-article230513334.

Chapter 5 – Service Without Reward

1 Valmai A. Hankel, 'Mortlock, John Andrew Tennant (1894–1950)', *Australian Dictionary of Biography*, National Centre of Biography, Australian National University, https://adb.edu.au/biography/mortlock-john-andrew-tennant-1182/text19927, accessed online 15 March 2022.

2   John Davis, 2014, *Principles & Pragmatism: Vol. 1, A History of Girton and King's College, the antecedents of Pembroke School*, Wakefield Press, Adelaide, pp. 20–21.
3   ibid., p. 115 and Concert By Students (May 2, 1933). *Advertiser*, p. 10. Retrieved November 3, 2021, from http://nla.gov.au/nla.news-article41482711.
4   See *St Mark's College Record. Special Supplement, The History of the College and College Register 1925–1935*. 1935, p. 27 at https://nla.gov.au:443/tarkine/nla.obj-2334397635. This is a 1935 photograph of the governors, staff and students of St Mark's College. Edward Hodgetts is fifth from the left in the second last row. Mariah Long, Senior Archives Officer, Special Collections, Barr Smith Library, University of Adelaide provided information about Edward and Mary's university studies.
5   See *A Brief History of St Mark's College* at https://stmarkscollege.com.au/about/history/#prettyphoto.
6   *St Mark's College Record,* op. cit., pp. 4–5 at https://nla.gov.au:443/tarkine/nla.obj-2334397635.
7   St Mark's College (February 14, 1930). *Advertiser*, p. 21. Retrieved November 3, 2021, from http://nla.gov.au/nla.news-article29009792.
8   See *St Mark's College Record.* op. cit., p. 27.
9   Davis, op. cit., pp. 42, 90, 104 and 120.
10 Davis, op. cit., pp. 35–39. Before she married, Mrs Irwin and her sister had run Merton Hall, a private-venture school in Melbourne. She did the bulk of the work to re-establish Girton. Her one regret was that she did not move the motion to continue the school at a public meeting held in October 1925. Her husband, the Rev. W.H. Irwin, moved it on her behalf. Patriarchy prevailed.
11 Davis, op. cit., pp. 38–41 and 49.
12 Davis, op. cit., pp. 58–59.
13 Davis, op. cit., p. 102.
14 Davis, op. cit., p. 86.
15 Davis, op. cit., pp. 86–87.
16 Davis, op. cit., pp. 109 and 111.
17 For examples of Hodgetts' involvement see St Mark's College (January 18, 1928). *Register*, p. 2. Retrieved November 10, 2021, from http://nla.gov.au/nla.news-article29009792; Girton School. Annual Inter-House Sports (July 27, 1929). *Advertiser*, p. 9. Retrieved November 3, 2021, from http://nla.gov.au/nla.news-article357524464; School Speech Days: Reports On Year's Work (December 19, 1933). *Advertiser*, p. 5. Retrieved November 3, 2021, from http://nla.gov.

au/nla.news-article74086969; and American Tea At Girton (April 7, 1934). *News*, p. 6. Retrieved November 4, 2021, from http://nla.gov.au/nla.news-article12885618.
18. Davis, op. cit., pp. 100–101.
19. Davis, op. cit., pp. 76–77.
20. Davis, op. cit., pp. 87–88.
21. General News. Citizens' League (October 11, 1930). *Advertiser*, p. 16. Retrieved March 22, 2022, from http://nla.gov.au/nla.news-article29840721; and Citizens' League (December 9, 1930). *Advertiser*, p. 10. Retrieved March 22, 2022, from http://nla.gov.au/nla.news-article29852768.
22. Political Reform League (March 12, 1930). *Advertiser*, p. 7. Retrieved March 17, 2022, from http://nla.gov.au/nla.news-article73791181.
23. Trevor Matthews, *The All for Australia League*, in Labour History, No. 17, October 1969, Liverpool University Press, p. 136.
24. Political Reform League (March 29, 1929). *Mount Barker Courier and Onkaparinga and Gumeracha Advertiser*, p. 8. Retrieved March 17, 2022, from http://nla.gov.au/nla.news-article147840596.
25. Liberal and Country League. Kensington Gardens Women's Branch (November 29, 1935). *Advertiser*, p. 34. Retrieved November 3, 2021, from http://nla.gov.au/nla.news-article36200311.
26. Boothby Election. Honoring Prime Minister (May 22, 1941). *Advertiser*, p. 13. Retrieved November 9, 2021, from http://nla.gov.au/nla.news-article74466533.
27. For a succinct account of Burke's theories about conservatism see Bryan Magee, 2001, *The Story of Philosophy*, Dorling Kindersley Limited, London, pp. 118–119.
28. Royal Institute For The Blind (October 9, 1931). *Kapunda Herald*, p. 4. Retrieved November 3, 2021, from http://nla.gov.au/nla.news-article108385302; and Blind Appeal 'S.O.S.' (October 23, 1931). *Advertiser*, p. 17. Retrieved November 3, 2021, from http://nla.gov.au/nla.news-article74372532.
29. Sportsmen To Help Blind (October 1, 1931). *Advertiser*, p. 6. Retrieved November 3, 2021, from http://nla.gov.au/nla.news-article29866521; Schools Help Blind Appeal (October 10, 1931). *Advertiser*, p. 16. Retrieved November 3, 2021, from http://nla.gov.au/nla.news-article29868141; Blind Appeal 'S.O.S.' (October 23 ,1931). *Advertiser*, p. 17. Retrieved November 3, 2021, from http://nla.gov.au/nla.news-article74372532; College Boys Help (October 30, 1931). *Advertiser*, p. 22. Retrieved November 3, 2021, from http://nla.gov.au/nla.news-article29871808; Helping The Blind Institute (December 4,

1931). *Advertiser*, p. 25. Retrieved November 3, 2021, from http://nla.gov.au/nla.news-article74368315; and Blind Appeal (December 15, 1931). *Advertiser*, p. 14. Retrieved November 3, 2021, from http://nla.gov.au/nla.news-article29880826.

30 Blind Appeal (December 15, 1931). *Advertiser*, p. 14. Retrieved November 3, 2021, from http://nla.gov.au/nla.news-article29880826; Sir John Melrose Appeal (December 21, 1938). *Advertiser*, p. 26. Retrieved November 3, 2021, from http://nla.gov.au/nla.news-article36602370; and Blind Need More Support (July 21, 1939). *Advertiser*, p. 25. Retrieved November 3, 2021, from http://nla.gov.au/nla.news-article74424492.

31 Blind Workers In Defence Jobs (September 25, 1944). *Advertiser*, p. 8. Retrieved November 3, 2021, from http://nla.gov.au/nla.news-article43221648.

32 Stock Exchange Patriotic Concert (July 17, 1915). *Mail*, p. 6. Retrieved November 8, 2021, from http://nla.gov.au/nla.news-article59392716; War Funds. Men's Tobacco Auxiliary (November 24, 1917). *Advertiser*, p. 9. Retrieved November 3, 2021, from http://nla.gov.au/nla.news-article5574812; River Fete and Continental (February 23, 1918). *Mail*, p. 3. Retrieved November 8, 2021, from http://nla.gov.au/nla.news-article63842724; College Athletics (April 30, 1923). *Register*, p. 5. Retrieved November 3, 2021, from http://nla.gov.au/nla.news-article64178248; Before The Public (March 29, 1926). *News*, p. 1 (home edition). Retrieved November 10, 2021, from http://nla.gov.au/nla.news-article129764011; St. Peter's College Annual Sports (May 12, 1928). *Observer*, p. 11. Retrieved November 3, 2021, from http://nla.gov.au/nla.news-article16481256; League of Nations (November 7, 1929). *News*, p. 18 (home edition). Retrieved November 4, 2021, from http://nla.gov.au/nla.news-article12887252; £3850 For Angorichina Hostel (May 20, 1932). *News*, p. 10. Retrieved November 3, 2021, from http://nla.gov.au/nla.news-article129050936; and Royal Visit Arrangements (March 15, 1934). *Advertiser*, p. 8. Retrieved November 3, 2021from http://nla.gov.au/nla.news-article47543630.

33 'St Mark's College Fete' (October 18, 1924). *Register*, p. 14. Retrieved November 3, 2021, from http://nla.gov.au/nla.news-article57896773; The Social Round. Fete Arranged (June 24, 1927). *Register*, p. 12. Retrieved October 28, 2021, from http://nla.gov.au/nla.news-article54266034; The Social Round. St Mary's Mission Dance (July 9, 1927). *Saturday Journal*, p. 10. Retrieved November 3, 2021, from http://nla.gov.au/nla.news-article199273936; 'Toc H.' (June 2, 1928). *Advertiser*, p. 19. Retrieved November 3, 2021, from http://nla.gov.au/nla.news-article49385986; Billiards Party For Miss Joan Hodgetts

(February 18, 1942). *News*, p. 5. Retrieved October 28, 2021, from http://nla.gov.au/nla.news-article131956198; Wedding Dates (July 23, 1940). *Advertiser*, p. 13. Retrieved November 3, 2021, from http://nla.gov.au/nla.news-article47205128; and Davis op. cit., p. 132. The State Library of South Australia has a photograph, PRG-1619-4-3A, of RAAF trainees in 1941. On the back of the photograph are the words, '"Charlie" James G. Hodgetts'. This is a reference to Hodgetts' youngest son, James Gwynne Hodgetts. Mary Hodgetts' war record can be seen at the Virtual War Memorial Australia site at https://vwma.org.au/explore/people/561048. Similarly, Gordon Hodgetts' war record can be seen at https://vwma.org.au/explore/people/604643 and James Hodgetts' at https://vwma.org.au/explore/people/511408.

Chapter 6 – Keeping Up Appearances

1 Alison Dolling, *A History of Kensington Gardens* in Burnside Historical Society Inc., Newsletter June, 1989, Volume 9, No. 2, p. 22.
2 In 1959, Vance Packard published *The Status Seekers*. Sociologists criticised Packard for drawing large inferences, writing from an upper-class perspective and for his argument lacking sound empirical evidence. Nevertheless, his essential thesis that many people aspire to upward social mobility holds in class-based, capitalist economic systems.
3 John Davis, 2014, *Principles & Pragmatism: Vol. 1, A History of Girton and King's College, the antecedents of Pembroke School*, Wakefield Press, Adelaide, pp. 90–97.
4 See entries for these men in *Who's Who: South Australia Centenary, 1936*, The Amalgamated Publishing Company, Adelaide, 1 September 1936. In *Secrets and ties: Just join the club*, Andrew Hough showed the exclusive nature of the Adelaide Club. Existing members invite applicants to apply for membership. The proposer must have a seconder and after a month the names of three other sponsors are revealed to members. Applicants may not lobby club members. The exact number of votes required to become a member is unknown. In the past, 10 'yes' votes had to be generated for every 'no' vote: nowadays the ratio is thought to be 4:1. Former Labor Premier John Bannon withdrew his application when it became clear he would be denied membership following a backlash over the collapse of the State Bank. The Club was forced to deny it was racist when Albert Bensimon, a prominent Adelaide jeweller, was denied membership. See Andrew Hough, *Advertiser*, 2 September 2022, pp. 21–22.

5   There is a photograph taken of Bishop Nutter Thomas and his wife, Mary, at Bishop's Court in 1906 in the *Chronicle*, 26 May 1906, p. 31. See also State Library of South Australia, Photograph B 64334.
6   *St Mark's College Record: Special Supplement: The History of The College and College Register*, 1925–1935, pp. 4–5; and P.A. Howell, 'Poole, Frederic Slaney (1845–1936)', *Australian Dictionary of Biography*, National Centre of Biography, Australian National University, https://adb.anu.edu.au/biography/poole-frederic-slaney-8075/text14093, accessed online 2 March 2023. Dorothea Poole, the third headmistress of Girton during Hodgetts' chairmanship of the Board, was Justice Thomas Poole's sister.
7   Davis, op. cit., pp. 9–10, 11 & 41–42.
8   Personal. (October 20, 1928). *Chronicle,* p. 49. Retrieved August 31, 2022, from http://nla.gov.au/nla.news-article87566534.
9   The Annual Battle Between The Blues And Reds Was Also A Social Event (July 31, 1930). *Observer,* p. 51. Retrieved August 31, 2022, from http://nla.gov.au/nla.news-article164798735. Archdeacon J.S. Moyes, brother of the legendary Australian cricket commentator Johnny Moyes, and the Rev. H.P. Finnis attended the lunch and both had historical links with Girton.
10 Adelaide. English Cricketers Entertained (November 23, 1929). *Australasian*, p. 14. Retrieved August 31, 2022, from http://nla.gov.au/nla.news-article141389711.
11 White Frocks Worn By Women At Cricket (January 25, 1937). *Advertiser*, p. 6. Retrieved August 31, 2022, from http://nla.gov.au/nla.news-article47779843. Details about the match between South Australia and the Marylebone Cricket Club were cited at http://static.espncricinfo.com/db/ARCHIVE/1930S/1936-37/ENG_IN_AUS/MCC_SOA_22-26JAN1937.html.
12 English Speaking Union Bridge (May 28, 1932). *Advertiser*, p. 14. Retrieved August 31, 2022, from http://nla.gov.au/nla.news-article46861834.
13 Catherine Clay, 2016, *British Women Writers 1914–1945: Professional Work and Friendship*, Routledge, Milton Park, Oxfordshire. Accessed online.
14 500 Attend Levee At Government House (June 10, 1938). *Advertiser*, p. 14. Retrieved August 31, 2022, from http://nla.gov.au/nla.news-article35587417.
15 An article in the *Mail*, 28 May 1932, p. 5, described the dress worn at Government House levees. See What to Wear at the Birthday Levee (May 28, 1932). *Mail*, p. 5 (Magazine Section). Retrieved August 31, 2022, from http://nla.gov.au/nla.news-article59307113.

16 The term *hoi polloi* was used to describe the masses, the common people, the general public. The ceremonial levee originated from the Court of French King, Louis XIV. To mark a clear distinction between the monarch and his aristocratic courtiers he established elaborate conventions whereby the full court assembled outside the king's bedchamber – the *petit lever* – as he dressed. Charles II adapted the system for England in the 17th century.
17 500 Attend Levee At Government House (June 10, 1938). *Advertiser*, p. 14. Retrieved August 31, 2022, from http://nla.gov.au/nla.news-article35587417.
18 ibid. Prominent identities in the General List included A.G. Ayers, Sirs Langdon and Lavington Bonython, G.H. Boucaut, A.M. Cudmore, F. Lloyd Dumas, F. Downer, Sir William Goodman, Professor Kerr Grant, C.H. De Crespigny, R.C. Gosse, A. O'Halloran Giles, A.S. Hawker, E.W. Hayward, Sir Douglas Mawson, Sir Henry Newland, A.C. Rymill, E.F. Scarfe, S. Talbot Smith, T. Barr Smith, Snr, T. Barr Smith, Jnr, and W.C.N. Waite.
19 Mr. and Mrs. H.W. Hodgetts Entertain (May 18, 1935). *Advertiser*, p. 12. Retrieved October 28, 2021, from http://nla.gov.au/nla.news-article37288856.
20 Billiards Party For Miss Joan Hodgetts (February 18, 1942). *News*, p. 5. Retrieved November 3, 2021, from http://nla.gov.au/nla.news-article131956198.
21 Toc H. (June 2, 1928). *Advertiser*, p. 19. Retrieved November 3, 2021, from http://nla.gov.au/nla.news-article49385986.
22 At Home For Captain Bertram (October 5, 1932). *Advertiser*, p. 10. Retrieved November 4, 2021, from article35170369. With his co-pilot, Adolph Klausemann, Bertram had attempted to fly a Junkers seaplane from Germany to Australia. Forced to abandon their plane near Cape Bernier, West Australia, on 24 May 1932, they were rescued on 28 June. The local Miwa people helped them survive their ordeal.
23 What People Are Doing (July 4, 1935). *News*, p. 14. Retrieved November 3, 2021, from http://nla.gov.au/nla.news-article128420845. Fifty-five women prominent in the arts and professions founded the Lyceum Club in 1922. Dr Helen Mayo was its first president. See *Lyceum Club* at https://www.lyceumadelaide.org.au/about/history-of-the-club.html.
24 Stock Exchange Ball. Social (August 12, 1938). *Advertiser*, p. 8. Retrieved November 4, 2021, from http://nla.gov.au/nla.news-article35604767.
25 Dance At St. Corantyn For Younger Set (December 18, 1935). *Advertiser*, p. 10. Retrieved November 4, 2021, from http://nla.gov.au/

nla.news-article36205317; and information located on plaques about St Corantyn provided by the City of Adelaide. Young men and women from the Melrose, Hawker, Simpson, Rymill, Angove, Downer, Dutton and other leading families attended the dance.

Chapter 7 – The Road to Ruin

1 Bankruptcy of H.W. Hodgetts (July 12, 1945). *Advertiser*, p. 7. Retrieved November 10, 2021, from http://nla.gov.au/nla.news-article43501705; and Rogues of the Stock Exchange (August 24, 1952). *Truth*, p. 14. Retrieved November 3, 2021, from http://nla.gov.au/nla.news-article168007621.

2 Roland Perry, From batting to broking in the *Financial Review*, online edition, 25 October 1996 at https://www.afr.com/politics/from-batting-to-broking-19961025-k75bi; and Roland Perry, 2019, *Tea and Scotch with Bradman*, HarperCollins Publishers, Australia Pty Limited for ABC Books, Sydney, p. 131. Perry interviewed Sir Donald Bradman for this book and may have based the time that the Broken Hill agent misappropriated funds on Sir Donald's recall of events that had occurred half a century earlier and the details of which he was unfamiliar.

3 Mr. A.E. Hall Leaving (September 29, 1928). *Barrier Miner*, p. 2. Retrieved December 21, 2021, from http://nla.gov.au/nla.news-article46035224; and T. Hall and Son (December 16, 1924). *Barrier Miner*, p. 3. Retrieved December 21, 2021, from http://nla.gov.au/nla.news-article45879939.

4 Mount Magnet Gold Claim (August 13, 1927). *Barrier Miner*, p. 1. Retrieved December 21, 2021, from http://nla.gov.au/nla.news-article45982582.

5 Mr. A.E. Hall Leaving (September 29, 1928). *Barrier Miner*, p. 2. Retrieved December 21, 2021, from http://nla.gov.au/nla.news-article46035224.

6 Alleged False Pretences (March 13, 1929). *Barrier Miner*, p. 1. Retrieved December 22, 2021, from http://nla.gov.au/nla.news-article46054081; Alleged False Pretences (March 14, 1929). *Advertiser*, p. 9. Retrieved December 22, 2021, from http://nla.gov.au/nla.news-article73731853; and Alleged False Pretences (March 14, 1929). *Sydney Morning Herald*, p. 12. Retrieved December 22, 2021, from http://nla.gov.au/nla.news-article16538195.

7 Alleged False Pretences (March 27, 1929). *Barrier Miner*, p. 3. Retrieved December 22, 2021, from http://nla.gov.au/nla.news-article46055745; Late Mr. A.E. Hall (March 28, 1929). *Barrier Miner*, p. 2. Retrieved December 22, 2021, from http://nla.gov.au/nla.

news-article46055859; The Late Mr. A.E. Hall (March 30, 1929). *Barrier Miner*, p. 2. Retrieved December 22, 2021, from http://nla.gov.au/nla. news-article46055939; and Accused Man Shot Dead (March 28 ,1929). *Register News-Pictorial*, p. 3. Retrieved December 22, 2021, from http://nla.gov.au/nla.news-article53473139.
8 Bankruptcy Court. Late A.E. Hall's Estate (September 9, 1930). *Barrier Miner*, p. 3. Retrieved December 22, 2021, from http://nla.gov.au/nla. news-article46552378.
9 Share Transactions (November 4 ,1932). *Advertiser*, p. 19. Retrieved December 21, 2021, from http://nla.gov.au/nla.news-article73993306; and Brokers To Pay £1,740 (December 16, 1932). *News*, p. 7. Retrieved December 21, 2021, from http://nla.gov.au/nla.news-article128939649.
10 ibid. and Verdict For J.T. Gorman (December 16 ,1932). *Barrier Miner)*, p. 1. Retrieved December 21, 2021, from http://nla.gov.au/nla.news-article46675472. The *Sydney Morning Herald* of Wednesday 6 March 1935 published an article on wages based on figures prepared by the Commonwealth Statistician. The average male national income in December 1932 was £212/15/4. Real Wages. (March 6, 1935). *Sydney Morning Herald*, p. 13. Retrieved December 21, 2021, from http://nla.gov.au/nla.news-article17143201.
11 Rogues of the Stock Exchange (August 24, 1952). *Truth (Sydney, NSW: 1894–1954)*, p. 14. Retrieved November 3, 2021, from http://nla.gov.au/nla.news-article168007621.
12 'Futures' are derivative financial contracts obliging a buyer to purchase an asset or a seller to sell an asset at a predetermined future date and set price.
13 R.M. Gibbs, 1988, *Bulls, Bears and Wildcats: A Centenary History of the Stock Exchange of Adelaide*, Peacock Publications, Norwood, pp. 198–199.
14 Bankruptcy of H.W. Hodgetts (July 12, 1945). *Advertiser*, p. 7. Retrieved October 28, 2021, from http://nla.gov.au/nla.news-article43501705; and Rogues of the Stock Exchange (August 24, 1952). *Truth*, p. 14. Retrieved November 3, 2021, from http://nla.gov.au/nla.news-article168007621.
15 Bankruptcy Case. Hodgetts In Third Day (August 9, 1945). *Advertiser*, p. 7. Retrieved November 3, 2021, from http://nla.gov.au/nla.news-article43505836.
16 R.M. Gibbs, op. cit., pp. 302–303; Bankruptcy of H.W. Hodgetts (July 12, 1945). *Advertiser*, p. 7. Retrieved August 31, 2022, from http://nla.gov.au/nla.news-article43501705; and No Privilege of Silence (August 7, 1945). *Newcastle Morning Herald and Miners' Advocate (NSW:*

1876–1954), p. 3. Retrieved August 31, 2022, from http://nla.gov.au/nla.news-article134357148.
17 Bankruptcy Case. Hodgetts In Third Day (August 9, 1945). *Advertiser*, p. 7. Retrieved November 3, 2021, from http://nla.gov.au/nla.news-article43505836.

Chapter 8 – Financial Folly and Failure

1 R.M. Gibbs, op. cit., p. 303.
2 ibid.
3 Hodgetts Estate Report By official Receiver (July 11, 1945). *News*, p. 1. Retrieved October 28, 2021, from http://nla.gov.au/nla.news-article130232011.
4 Bankruptcy Case. Hodgetts In Third Day (August 9, 1945). *Advertiser*, p. 7. Retrieved November 3, 2021, from http://nla.gov.au/nla.news-article43505836.
5 Suzanne Edgar, 'Melrose, Alexander (1865–1944)', *Australian Dictionary of Biography, National Centre of Biography*, Australian National University, https://adb.anu.edu.au/biography/melrose-alexander-11105/text19771, accessed online 4 May 2022.
6 Out Among The People. Progress At Darwin (January 4, 1940). *Chronicle,* p. 58. Retrieved November 3, 2021, from http://nla.gov.au/nla.news-article92387186.
7 Bankruptcy of H.W. Hodgetts (July 12, 1945). *Advertiser*, p. 7. Retrieved October 28, 2021, from http://nla.gov.au/nla.news-article43501705.
8 Hodgetts Arrested At Home In Bed (July 14 ,1945). *News*, p. 1. Retrieved October 28, 2021, from http://nla.gov.au/nla.news-article130237590.
9 Gibbs, op. cit., pp. 292–293.
10 ibid.
11 Gibbs, op. cit., p. 303.
12 Roland Perry, 2019, *Tea and Scotch with Bradman*, HarperCollins Publishers, Australia Pty Limited for ABC Books, Sydney, p. 132.
13 Hodgetts Case Creditors Meet (July 19 1945). *Advertiser*, p. 3. Retrieved November 3, 2021, from http://nla.gov.au/nla.news-article43502659.
14 Bankruptcy Hodgetts Case In Third Day (August 9 1945). *Advertiser*, p. 7. Retrieved November 3, 2021, from http://nla.gov.au/nla.news-article43505836.
15 ibid.; and Hodgetts Knew Position Bad, But Was Hopeful (August 8, 1945). *Herald*, p. 3. Retrieved October 28, 2021, from http://nla.gov.au/nla.news-article249157378.

16 Rogues of the Stock Exchange (August 24, 1952). *Truth*, p. 14. Retrieved November 3, 2021, from http://nla.gov.au/nla.news-article168007621.
17 Banker On Loan To Hodgetts (August 17, 1945). *News*, p. 3. Retrieved October 27, 2021, from http://nla.gov.au/nla.news-article130237007.
18 Broker's Failure (July 12, 1945). *West Australian*, p. 6. Retrieved October 28, 2021, from http://nla.gov.au/nla.news-article51757788.
19 About People (September 25 ,1944). *Advertiser*, p. 8. Retrieved November 3, 2021, from http://nla.gov.au/nla.news-article43221608.
20 Bankruptcy of H.W. Hodgetts (July 12, 1945). *Advertiser*, p. 7. Retrieved October 28, 2021, from http://nla.gov.au/nla.news-article43501705.
21 ibid.
22 ibid.
23 Gibbs, op. cit., p. 302; and Bradman On Change (May 13, 1943). *Northern Star*, p. 5. Retrieved October 28, 2021, from http://nla.gov.au/nla.news-article96422153. Viner Smith made the announcement as the President, Andrew Young, was attending a conference in Melbourne. In *The Don's War*, in the *Sydney Morning Herald*, 23 September 2012, Malcolm Knox explained that Bradman had trained at Frankston, Victoria, as a physical education instructor for the army. Bradman suffered from fibrositis, was hospitalised three times and was discharged on the grounds of ill health in June 1941. After convalescing at Bowral he resumed his work as a broker's clerk at H.W. Hodgetts & Co. in 1942.
24 Broker's Estate Sequestrated (June 4, 1945). *Advertiser*, p. 2. Retrieved October 28, 2021, from http://nla.gov.au/nla.news-article43495926.

Chapter 9 – Public Shame

1 R.M. Gibbs, 1988, *Bulls, Bears and Wildcats: A Centenary History of the Stock Exchange of Adelaide*, Peacock Publications, Norwood, p. 302.
2 Bankruptcy of Sharebroker (June 5, 1945). *Advertiser*, p. 2. Retrieved August 31, 2022, from http://nla.gov.au/nla.news-article43496086.
3 R.M. Gibbs, op. cit., p. 302; Richard Brook, *'The Don' accused of underarm tactics in financial scandal*, nzherald.com.nz, 23 November 2001 at https://www.nzherald.co.nz/sport/cricket-the-don-accused-of-underarm-tactics-in-financial-scandal; and David Dunstan and Tom Heenan, 'Shattering the Don Bradman myth', *New Daily*, 28 January 2014 at https://www.nzherald.co.nz/sport/cricket-the-don-accused-of-underarm-tactics-in-financial-scandal.
4 Bankruptcy of H.W. Hodgetts (July 12, 1945). *Advertiser*, p. 7. Retrieved October 28, 2021, from http://nla.gov.au/nla.news-article43501705.

5 ibid.
6 Hodgetts Estate Report (July 11, 1945). *News*, p. 1. Retrieved October 28, 2021, from http://nla.gov.au/nla.news-article130232011.
7 Gibbs, op. cit., pp. 304–305.
8 Hodgetts' Estate Creditors Listed (July 7, 1945). *News*, p. 1. Retrieved June 4, 2021, from http://nla.gov.au/nla.news-article130234725; and Deficiency of £82,854 (July 11, 1945). *Weekly Times*, p. 4. Retrieved August 28, 2021, from http://nla.gov.au/nla.news-article226558760.
9 Arrested Man at Court (July 14, 1945). *News*, p. 1. Retrieved August 28, 2021, from http://nla.gov.au/nla.news-article13023759.
10 Bankruptcy Hodgetts Case In Third Day (August 9, 1945). *Advertiser*, p. 7. Retrieved November 3, 2021, from http://nla.gov.au/nla.news-article43505836.
11 Hodgetts Knew Position Bad, But Was Hopeful (August 8, 1945). *Herald (Melbourne, Vic.: 1861–1954)*, p. 3. Retrieved August 25, 2022, from http://nla.gov.au/nla.news-article249157378.
12 ibid.
13 Banker On Loan To Hodgetts (August 17, 1945). *News*, p. 3. Retrieved October 27, 2021, from http://nla.gov.au/nla.news-article130237007.
14 Hodgetts May Go Direct To Supreme Court (August 27, 1945). *News*, p. 1. Retrieved August 27, 2021, from http://nla.gov.au/nla.news-article130233197.
15 Lord Gowrie Creditor of H.W. Hodgetts (July 13, 1945). *Sydney Morning Herald*, p. 4. Retrieved October 28, 2021, from http://nla.gov.au/nla.news-article17947065.
16 Hodgetts May Go Direct To Supreme Court (August 27, 1945). *News*, p. 1. Retrieved August 27, 2021, from http://nla.gov.au/nla.news-article130233197.
17 Law Courts (September 11, 1945). *Advertiser*, p. 3. Retrieved August 25, 2022, from http://nla.gov.au/nla.news-article48667070.
18 Defrauder, In Gaol (September 9, 1945). *Truth (Sydney, NSW: 1894–1954)*, p. 15. Retrieved November 10, 2021, from http://nla.gov.au/nla.news-article169363485.
19 ibid.
20 ibid.
21 Hodgetts Gets 5 Years (September 10, 1945). *News*, p. 1. Retrieved August 27, 2021, from http://nla.gov.au/nla.news-article130233626.
22 Hodgetts in Tears, Five Years Gaol (September 11, 1945). *Border Watch (Mount Gambier, SA: 1861–1954)*, p. 1. Retrieved August 27, 2021, from http://nla.gov.au/nla.news-article78095816.

Chapter 10 – Fallout

1 Brett Hutchins, 2002, *Don Bradman: Challenging the Myth*, Cambridge University Press, Cambridge, p. 155.
2 R.M. Patching, 2014, *The Private Lives of Australian Cricket Stars*, Thesis submitted for the Degree of Doctor of Philosophy, Bond University, p. 163.
3 R.M. Gibbs, 1988, *Bulls, Bears and Wildcats: A Centenary History of the Stock Exchange of Adelaide*, Peacock Publications, Norwood, p. 305.
4 *South Australian Parliamentary Debates*, Session 1945, Thursday 19 July–21 December 1945, Government Printer, Adelaide, pp. 398 and 439–441.
5 *Commonwealth of Australia: Parliamentary Debates*, Senate and House of Representatives, Vol. 183, Wednesday, 18 July 1945, p. 4168; and Clyde Cameron, 'Chambers, Cyril (1897–1975)', *Australian Dictionary of Biography*, National Centre of Biography, Australian National University, https://adb.anu.edu.au/biography/chambers-cyril-972/text17165, accessed online 6 July 2022.
6 As Treasurer in John Curtin's Labor Government, Chifley had overseen the control of the economy during World War II. Following Curtin's premature death, he was elected Prime Minister on 13 July 1945, five days before he responded to Chambers' question in the House of Representatives.
7 *Commonwealth of Australia: Parliamentary Debates*, Senate and House of Representatives, Vol. 183, op. cit., pp. 4168–4169.
8 Gibbs, op. cit., p. 304.
9 Gibbs, op. cit., p. 305.
10 Hodgetts Case Creditors Meet (July 19, 1945). *Advertiser*, p. 3. Retrieved November 3, 2021, from http://nla.gov.au/nla.news-article43502659.
11 *Commonwealth of Australia Gazette*, Thursday 2 December 1948 (No. 163), p. 4140.
12 Directions given in Hodgetts' estate (January 14, 1949). *News*, p. 12. Retrieved October 28, 2021, from http://nla.gov.au/nla.news-article130244554.
13 *Commonwealth of Australia Gazette*, Thursday 9 June 1949 (No. 40), p. 1690.
14 Supreme Court: Woman Recovers Shares (July 21, 1951). *Advertiser*, p. 4. Retrieved October 28, 2021, from http://nla.gov.au/nla.news-article45719757.
15 R.M. Gibbs, op. cit., p. 304. Robert Martin, 1987, *Under Mount Lofty: A history of the Stirling District in South Australia*, Griffin Press, Netley,

p. 162 refers to Fisher living at Pine Hill, a stately home built by his father.
16. Roland Perry, 2019, *Tea and Scotch with Bradman*, HarperCollins Publishers, Australia Pty Limited for ABC Books, Sydney, p. 134.
17. Cited in Malcolm Knox, 2015, *Bradman's War: How the 1948 Invincibles Turned the Cricket Pitch into a Battlefield*, Penguin Random House Australia, Melbourne, p. 24.
18. ibid.
19. Roland Perry, From batting to broking in *Financial Review*, online edition, 25 October 1996 at https://www.afr.com/politics/from-batting-to-broking-19961025-k75bi.
20. Roland Perry, 2019, *Tea and Scotch with Bradman*, HarperCollins Publishers, Australia Pty Limited for ABC Books, Sydney, p. 134.
21. Gibbs, op. cit., p. 304.
22. Bankruptcy of Sharebroker (June 5, 1945). *Advertiser*, p. 2. Retrieved November 3, 2021, from http://nla.gov.au/nla.news-article43496086.
23. Knox, op. cit., p. 24.
24. Roland Perry, From batting to broking in *Financial Review*, op. cit.
25. Bradman Director of 5 Firms (February 29, 1948). *Sun*, p. 3. Retrieved January 28, 2022, from http://nla.gov.au/nla.news-article229040668.
26. Australians In New Year List: Bradman Gets Knighthood (January 1, 1949). *Sydney Morning Herald*, p. 1. Retrieved January 28, 2022, from http://nla.gov.au/nla.news-article32152836.
27. Richard Brook, *Cricket: 'The Don' accused of underarm tactics in financial scandal* in *New Zealand Herald*, 23 November 2001 online at https://www.nzherald.co.nz/sport/cricket-the-don-accused-of-underarm-tactics-in-financial-scandal.
28. Roland Perry, 2019, *Tea and Scotch with Bradman*, op. cit., p. 137.
29. Tom Heenan and David Dunstan, *Don Bradman: Just a boy from Bowral* in Bateman, Anthony & Hill, Jeffrey, (eds), 2011, *The Cambridge Companion to Cricket*, Cambridge University Press, Cambridge, pp. 94–95.
30. Roland Perry, From batting to broking in *Financial Review*, op. cit.
31. Tom Heenan and David Dunstan, *Don Bradman: Just a boy from Bowral*, op. cit; and *Oh what a lovely war – or was it?* at https://www.tandfonline.com/doi/abs/; and Knox, op. cit., p. 25.
32. David Dunstan and Tom Heenan, *Shattering the Don Bradman Myth* in *New Daily*, 28 January 2014 online at https://thenewdaily.com.au/sport/cricket/2014/01/28/shattering-bradman-myth/.

33 Brett Hutchins, 2002, *Don Bradman: Challenging the myth*, Cambridge University Press, Port Melbourne, p. 86; and *Sydney Morning Herald*, Monday 28 June 1954, p. 1 and Tuesday 29 June 1954, p. 5.
34 See online https://en.wikipedia.org/wiki/Yatala_Labour_Prison.
35 John Davis, 2014, *Principles & Pragmatism: Vol. 1, A History of Girton and King's College, the antecedents of Pembroke School*, Wakefield Press, p. 131.
36 Detectives Visit Former Stock Broker In Gaol (January 22, 1947). *Daily Examiner*, p. 3. Retrieved October 28, 2021, from http://nla.gov.au/nla.news-article195292545; and Prisoner Questioned on Gold Fraud (January 22, 1947). *Newcastle Morning Herald and Miners' Advocate*, p. 5. Retrieved October 28, 2021, from http://nla.gov.au/nla.news-article132866833.
37 *Australian Women's Weekly*, 22 January 1949, p. 19.
38 Gibbs, op. cit., p. 304.
39 Broker-Gambler is Now in Death's Shadow, August 3, (1947). *Truth*, p. 36. Retrieved October 28, 2021, from http://nla.gov.au/nla.news-article168779126.
40 Death at 67 of Mr. H.W. Hodgetts (October 5, 1949). *News*, p. 20. Retrieved October 28, 2021, from http://nla.gov.au/nla.news-article131233819.
41 Rogues of the Stock Exchange (August 24, 1952). *Truth*, p. 14. Retrieved November 3, 2021, from http://nla.gov.au/nla.news-article168007621.

Epilogue

1 Roland Perry, From batting to broking in *Financial Review*, online edition, 25 October 1996 at https://www.afr.com/politics/from-batting-to-broking-19961025-k75bi. Thomas Hardy's book *The Mayor of Casterbridge: The Life and Death of a Man of Character* was published in 1886.
2 Michael Neill, *Shakespeare's Tragedies* in Margareta De Grazia & Stanley Wells (eds), 2013, *The New Cambridge Companion To Shakespeare*, Cambridge University Press, Cambridge, p. 121.
3 Stuart Macintyre, *Class*, in Graeme Davison, John Hirst & Stuart Macintyre (eds), 1998, *The Oxford Companion To Australian History*, Oxford University Press, Melbourne, pp. 130–132.
4 Michael Young, 1994, *The Rise of the Meritocracy*, Routledge, Milton Park, Oxfordshire.
5 R.M. Gibbs, 1988, *Bulls, Bears and Wildcats: A Centenary History of the Stock Exchange of Adelaide*, Peacock Publications, Norwood,

pp. 25 & 54; The Rev. B.G. Edwards. (1888, September 18). *Express and Telegraph*, p. 3 (2nd edn). Retrieved August 31, 2022, from http://nla.gov.au/nla.news-article207753368; The Rev. B.G. Edwards' Share Transactions. (1888, October 20). *Kadina and Wallaroo Times*, p. 3. Retrieved August 31, 2022, from http://nla.gov.au/nla.news-article109098491; and The Rev. B.G. Edwards. (1889, October 25). *Petersburg Times*, p. 4. Retrieved August 31, 2022, from http://nla.gov.au/nla.news-article109494360.

6 'Pig Iron Bob' and the 1938 Port Kembla strike at https://www.atui.org.au/union-history-blog/0yvzc5r3utcit9u1p64lqg94w9pum3.

Acknowledgements

Several people fleshed out for me important details and for their help I am most grateful. Lacrosse South Australia's historian, Luke Oswald, helped me understand, at least a little, the intricacies of his sport. Pembroke School Archivist, Peta Harries, St Peter's College School Archivist, Andrea McKinnon-Matthews, and Senior Archives Officer, Special Collections, Barr Smith Library, University of Adelaide, Mariah Long, provided attendance dates of members of the Gwynne and Hodgetts families at their institutions. Michelle Smith, Research and Information Services Manager of Norman Waterhouse Solicitors, provided important information about Hodgetts' lawyer, William Ashley Norman. I thank Michelle Toft, Historical and Cultural Officer, City of Burnside, for helping to locate photographs of Carlshurst, and its current owners, Andrea and David Crase, for providing photos and allowing their use. Andrea also provided important information regarding the transfer of Carlshurst's ownership to Hodgetts. I thank the excellent staff of the State Library of South Australia for their assistance. I am most grateful to Michael Bollen and his wonderful team at Wakefield Press. I thank typesetter Michael Deves for his work on the text and producing such an attractive cover, and I especially thank my meticulous editor, Julia Beaven, who massaged and polished my writing with her keen eye and attention to detail. I am much indebted to my wife, Julie, for her forbearance during the writing of this book and for reviewing the manuscript.

John Davis

Resources

References

Davis, John, 2014, *Principles & Pragmatism: Vol. 1, A History of Girton and King's College, the antecedents of Pembroke School*, 2nd edn, Wakefield Press, Adelaide.

Davison, Graeme, Hurst, John & Macintyre, Stuart, 1998, *The Oxford Companion To Australian History*, Oxford University Press, Melbourne.

Davison, Graeme, 1978, *The Rise and Fall of Marvellous Melbourne*, Melbourne University Press, Carlton.

Frith, David, 2002, *Bodyline Autopsy: The Full Story of the most sensational Test Cricket series: Australia v England 1932–1933*, ABC Books, Sydney.

Gibbs, R.M., 1988, *Bulls, Bears and Wildcats: A Centenary History of the Stock Exchange of Adelaide*, Peacock Publications, Norwood.

Heenan, Tom and Dunstan, David, *Don Bradman: Just a boy from Bowral* in Bateman, Anthony & Hill, Jeffrey, (eds), 2011, *The Cambridge Companion to Cricket*, Cambridge University Press, Cambridge.

Hutchins, Brett, 2002, *Don Bradman: Challenging the Myth*, Cambridge University Press, Cambridge.

Knox, Malcolm, 2015, *Bradman's War: How the 1948 Invincibles Turned the Cricket Pitch into a Battlefield*, Penguin Random House Australia, Melbourne.

Magee, Bryan, 2001, *The Story of Philosophy*, Dorling Kindersley Limited, London.

Martin, Robert, 1987, *Under Mount Lofty: A history of the Stirling District in South Australia*, Griffin Press, Netley.

Neill, Michael, *Shakespeare's Tragedies* in De Grazia, Margareta & Wells, Stanley (eds), 2013, *The New Cambridge Companion To Shakespeare*, Cambridge University Press, Cambridge.

Perry, Roland, 2021, *Bradman Vs Bodyline: The inside story of the most notorious Ashes series in history*, Allen & Unwin, Crows Nest.

Perry, Roland, 2019, *Tea and Scotch with Bradman*, HarperCollins Publishers, Australia Pty Limited for ABC Books, Sydney.

Thomas, Jan (ed.), 1997, *South Australian Births Index of Registration 1842 to 1906*, Vol. 4 H, South Australian Genealogy & Heraldry Society Inc., South Australia.

van Dissel, Dirk, *The Adelaide Gentry, 1850–1920*, in Richards, Eric (ed.), 1986, *The Flinders History of South Australia, Social History*, Wakefield Press, Netley.

Warburton, Elizabeth, 1981, *The Paddocks Beneath, A History of Burnside from the Beginning*, Corporation of the City of Burnside, Adelaide.

Who's Who: South Australia Centenary, 1936, The Amalgamated Publishing Company, Adelaide.

Theses

McDonald, Peter F., 1972, *Age at First Marriage and Proportions Marrying in Australia 1860–1971*, Australian National University.

Patching, R.M., 2014, *The Private Lives of Australian Cricket Stars*, Bond University.

Directories

Sands & McDougall's South Australian Directories, Sands and McDougall, Adelaide.

Newspapers and journals

Advertiser

Australasian

Australian Home Beautiful

Australian Women's Weekly

Australian Worker

Avon Argus and Cunderdin-Meckering-Tammin Mail (WA)

Barrier Miner

Border Watch (Mount Gambier)

Burnside Historical Society Inc., Newsletter June, 1989, Vol. 9, No. 2.

Chronicle

Commonwealth of Australia Gazette

Commonwealth of Australia: Parliamentary Debates, Senate and House of Representatives, Vol. 183, 13 June 1945–19 July 1945.

Daily Examiner (Grafton, NSW)

Daily Mercury (McKay, Qld)

Daily Standard

Evening Journal

Examiner

Express and Telegraph

Herald (Melbourne)

Kapunda Herald

Labour History, No. 17, October 1969, Liverpool University Press, Liverpool.

Mail

Manning River Times and Advocate for the Northern Coast Districts of New South Wales

Mount Barker Courier and Onkaparinga Advertiser

Newcastle Morning Herald and Miners' Advocate

News

Observer

Referee

Register

Register News-Pictorial

Saturday Journal

Scone Advocate (NSW)

South Australian Parliamentary Debates, Session 1945, Thursday 19 July–21 December 1945

St Mark's College Record: Special Supplement: The History of the College and College Register, 1925–1935.

Sun (Sydney)

Sydney Morning Herald

Telegraph

Truth (Sydney)

Weekly Times (Melbourne)

West Australian

Online links

Readers can access online articles using the addresses located in the endnotes.

Sources of photographs, images and illustrations

Andrea and David Crase, current owners of Carlshurst

Australian Home Beautiful

Australian Women's Weekly

Barrier Miner

News

Referee (Sydney)

South Australian Homes & Gardens

St Mark's College, 1935, St Mark's College record. Special supplement, the history of the college and college register 1925–1935

State Library of South Australia

Sun (Sydney)

Telegraph (Brisbane)
Truth (Sydney)
Who's Who: South Australia Centenary, 1936, The Amalgamated Publishing Company, Adelaide

Index

Numbers in *italic* indicate illustrations.

A
Abbott, Charles 107
Accrington Cricket Club 45
Adelaide Club 5, 6, 44, 71, 77, *77*, 88, 100, 105
Club debentures 90, 100
Adelaide Establishment. See Adelaide Gentry
Adelaide gentry
　Adelaide Club 5, 6, 88
　families 4, 5, 26, 72, 88
　female accomplishments 6
　lifestyle 6, 22
　links to the Church of England 71
　schooling 6, 71
　service ethic 52
Adelaide Hunt Club 6
Adelaide Oval 1, 37, *38*, 41, 43, 73, *74*, 120
Adelaide Police Court 98, 102

Advertiser Newspapers Ltd 24
Angas Parsons, Justice Herbert 71, 76, 82, *82*, 83
Angorichina Tuberculosis Hostel 68
Angove, Dorothy 56, 58, 62, 63, 73
　relations with Girton Board of Directors 61
Associated Newspapers 45
Australian Board of Control for International Cricket 31, 37, 47, 105
　'Bodyline' issue 39
Australian Wheat Board 84

B
Badcock, Jack 42–43
Bagot, Captain E.D.A. 62–63
Bakewell, William 71
Bank of Adelaide 91, 97, 101, 103, 107

Bankruptcy Court 80, 91, 94, 95, 98, 99, 101, 110
Barclay-Harvey, Sir Malcolm 23
Barwell, Sir Henry 73
Belgian Relief Fund 18
Beresford, Miss Sydney 78
Bickersteth, Rev. Kenneth Julian Faithfull 54
Bishop, Edith 56
  dispute with John Dempster 62–62
Blanchetown Post Office 9
Blanchetown Primary School 9, 66
bodyline bowling 38, 39
bonds 18, 24, 89, 103
Bonython, John Langdon 52, 63–64
Bonython, Lady 79
Bonython, Lavington 73
Bowral 44
Bradman, Donald George
  and consequences of Hodgetts's failure 112–115
  breach of contract with the Australian Board of Control 45
  critical views of 46–48, 124
  early employment outside cricket 44, 45, 46
  education of 44
  establishing his own stockbroking company, 94, 95
  immersed in cricket 46
  importance of work outside cricket 44

journalism 46
knighthood 113
meeting clients of H.W. Hodgetts & Co. 44
negotiations with Accrington Cricket Club 45
other brokers' resentment of 112–115
personal qualities 43, 46
positive newspaper reporting of his move to Adelaide 49
reaction to his move to Adelaide 49–50
relationship with teammates and opponents 46
relationship with the Australian Board of Control for International Cricket 45, 47
relocating to Adelaide 48–49
replaces Hodgetts on Australian Board of Control for International Cricket 115, 124
retires from stockbroking 115
salary at H.W. Hodgetts & Co. 41
success as a batsman prior to 1934 41–42
terms of the deal to transfer to South Australia 41
Bradman, Jessie (nee Menzies) 45, 48, *49*, *51*, 68, 111, 115
  as 'Mrs Don Bradman' 75
Brighton Cement Works 25
Broken Hill 80, 81, 82, 123
Broken Hill Chamber of Commerce 81

Broken Hill South Mining Company 24, 102, 110
brokers, *see also* sharebrokers and stockbrokers 18, 19, 24, 26, 89, 92, 94, 96–97, 106–107, 112, 113, 114, 115
  advertising regulations 20, 23, 44
  affected by Hodgetts' bankruptcy 94, 106, 109, 124
  alleged malpractices 83, 97, 108, 123
  compulsory audits of books 97, 108
  frequented hotels 19
  Great Depression 25–26
  involvement in sport 19, 29
  jargon 18
  lack of auditing 96, 106–107
  licensing 107
  loyalty to the British Empire 22
  speculative practices 84
  trading 15, 18
  trust accounts 107
Brookman, George 19
Brown, J.L. 42
Brownsword, John 19
Bruce, Theodore 19
Bullock, Len 112, 113, 115
Burns, G.W., Official Receiver 80, 97, 109, 110, 113
  imposed conditions on Bradman 112
  lack of regulations controlling brokers' practices 95–96
  reasons for Hodgetts's failure 92
Burnside 6, 64, 78
Burnside Post Office 9
Burra 66

C

Carlshurst. See Lichfield
Carr, Whitmore 18, 19, 24
Chamber of Commerce 89
Chamber of Manufactures 109
Chamberlain, R.R., Crown Prosecutor 103
Chambers, Cyril, MP 107–108
Chapple, Charlie 19
Chifley, Ben 108
Chomley, Ella Mildred 23, 97, 102, 110, 111
Church of England 57, 58, 59, 71, 73
Citizens' League 62–63
Civil Court 82–83, 110
community service 52–69 *passim*
Cook, Edith 6
Coolgardie 27
Cowra Chambers 19, 20, *20*, 57, 109
Cush, Frank 50

D

Darnley Naylor, Professor Henry 72
Darwin 28, 88, 89, 123
Darwin Hotel syndicate 27, 123
Darwin hotels 27–28, 88
Daws, Chief Inspector Wilfred 117
Dempster, John 61–62

Dolling, Dr C.E. 49
Dolling, Mrs D.B.C. 97
Don Bradman & Co. 95, 114
Downer family 54
Downer, Frank *74*
Downer, Sir John 55
Dugan, Sir Winston Joseph 74, 76
Duncan-Hughes, John 71
Dwyer, 'Chappie' 31

E
East Adelaide Lacrosse Club 30
East End Market Company 25
East Torrens Cricket Club 31, 34, 36, 37
East Torrens Lacrosse Club 30, 34–35, 35
education of Hodgetts' children 23, 53–54
Edward Ward & Co. 107
Egerton-Warburton, Mrs W. 4
Elder Smith & Company 26
Emergency Committee 63
English public schools 54
  influence on Australian schools' values 53
English Speaking Union 75

F
Farr, Marion 102, 110
Felt & Textile Limited 24, 102
Fisher, Guy 23, 88, 90, 97, 99, 100, 110, 111
F.J. Palmer & Son 41, 45, 46
Forbes, Registrar of Bankruptcy Court 99

Fotheringham, Tony 19
Fowler, David 55
Fowler, James 55
Fowler, Laura 6

G
Geelong Football Club 66
General Motors 25
George Wills & Co. 49
Giffen, George 37
Girton 1, 23, 58–59, *59*, 61, 63, 65, 68, 69, 71, 72, 78, 116
  Board of Directors 2, 56
  Girton House Girls' Grammar School 57
  Girton Proprietary Ltd 23, *57*
  Girton Proprietary School for Girls 53
  founding of 57–58
  Mothers' Association 60
  Old Scholars' Association 68
Glenelg Golf Club 66
Glynde Place 4, 5, 7, *7*
gold standard 25–26
Goldsborough Mort & Co. 24, 102
Good, H.M. 15
Gorman, John Thomas *82*, 82–83, 84, 123
Gosse, James 49, 71
Government House 6, 73, 75
  levee at 75–77
Grant, Roberta 117
Great Depression 24–26, 45, 58, 80

Index

Grenfell Price, Sir Archibald 54, 55, 56, 59, 63, 64, 72
Grimmett, Clarence Victor ('Clarrie') 32, 42, 43
Gwynne, Charles George Gordon 5
Gwynne, ('Edith') Mary Edith Gordon
  family background and early life 6, 7, 11, 12
  see also Hodgetts, ('Edith') Mary Edith Gordon
Gwynne, Edward Castres Snr 5, 11
Gwynne, Edward Castres Jnr 5
Gwynne, Edward Castres Mortlock 5

H

Hall, Allan Edward 81, 82, 83, 84, 86, 123, 124
Hawker, David 97
Hawker, Edward 71
Hawker, Mrs A. 97
Henley Croquet Club 66
Heuzenroeder, S.W. 81
Hill, Clem 19, 31, 49
Hodgetts, Charles 9, 22
Hodgetts, ('Edith') Mary Edith Gordon 4–5, 12, 52, 97
  annual allowance 22, 90
  as 'Mrs H.W. Hodgetts' 74, 77, 78, 79
  guarantor of H.W. Hodgetts' estate 110–111
  Liberal and Country League 64
  service to the community 59–60, 68, 75
  social activities 73, 75, 78
  visiting her husband in gaol 116
Hodgetts, Edward ('Ted') 11, 23, 53, 54, 78, 79
Hodgetts, Emily Armit 8
Hodgetts, Ethel 9
Hodgetts, Florence 9
Hodgetts, Henry ('Gordon') 11, 23, 53, 78, 79
  war service 68–69
Hodgetts, Henry ('Harry') Warburton Jnr
  a 'bad knock' 80, 82
  affluent lifestyle 22, 70, 71, 121
  a 'hands on' school chairman 59, 59
  arrest of 98
  assets and liabilities at time of collapse 91, 92, 97, 103
  a wily operator 51
  bankruptcy 92, 93, 94, 96, 106, 112, 113
  before the Bankruptcy Court 80, 94, 98–99
  Chairman and President, South Australian Lacrosse Association 35
  Chairman, Girton's Board of Directors 2, 53, 56, 58, 72
  Chairman, Kensington District Cricket Club 36
  charges against at trial 102–103
  clerk in the Adelaide General Post Office 11, 13

conservative political affiliations 63–64, 88
conviction and sentence 2, 105, 116
creditors of 90, 93, 94, 97, 109, 110, 115
cricket player 31
death of 117–118
effects of a 'bad knock' 83–84
failure of his Broken Hill agent 81–83
family background and early life 8–12
family homes in Kensington Park 21–22
financial folly and failure 87–93 *passim*
getting Bradman to Adelaide 41–48 *passim*
illegal practices 2, 87, 95, 96, 102, 106, 107, 124
illness at time of arrest 94, 97, 98, 101
incarceration in Yatala Labour Prison 116
irregular bookkeeping 85, 95–96
J.T. Gorman case 82–83, *82*
lacrosse player 30–31
pleaded guilty at trial 2, 103, 105, 124
President, Kensington Oval Citizens' Improvement Committee 33
President, South Australian Olympic Council 34, 105
prosperous appearance of 43
public profile 73, 86
role in founding St Mark's College 55–56
secretary of The Stock Exchange of Adelaide 11, 14–19
sequestration of assets 95, 99, 100, 103
service to Girton 2, 56–62 *passim*
service to lacrosse 34–36
service to The Royal Institute for the Blind 65–67, *65*, 88, 91, 102, 103
service to the South Australian Cricket Association 37, 42
service to St Peter's College 67
size of his financial scandal 106
social aspirations 12, 14, 53–54, 70–78 *passim*, 86, 109
South Australian delegate to the Australian Board of Control for International Cricket 37, 105
sports administrator 29, 32–40 *passim*
student at St Peter's College *10*, 11
trial of 94, 102–105
Hodgetts, Henry Warburton Snr 8–9, 11
Hodgetts, James 11, 23, 53, 79
war service 68–69
Hodgetts, Joan 11, 23, 53, 78
war service 68–69
Hodgetts, Mary 11, 23, 53, 54, 68
war service 68

Index

Hodgetts, Richard 9
Hodgetts Trust Account 97
Holden, Sir Edward 73
Holden's Motor Body Builders 25
Hore-Ruthven, Lady Zara. See also Lady Gowrie 59, *85*
Hore-Ruthven, Sir Alexander. See also Lord Gowrie 23, 73, *85*
Hotel Darwin 88
Hughes, Mrs E.B. 78
Hughes, Mrs L.M.A. 97
Hughes, Sir Walter 52
H.W. Hodgetts & Co. 20, *20*, 41, 57, 69, 87
  clients of 20, 23, 43, 44, 69, 85, 87, 89, 90, 92, 95, 96, 101,110, 112, 113
  financial difficulties of 80, 82, 83, 94

I
Irwin, Mrs W.H. 57, 61
Isaachsen, Oscar 91, 101

J
Jamestown 66
Japanese bomb Darwin 88, 89, 123
Jardine, Douglas 38–39
Jeanes, W.H. 31
Jeffcott, Sir John 11
Johnson, Richard 82

K
Kalgoorlie 19, 27, 117
Kapunda Lacrosse Club 35
Kelly, William 39

Kensington District Cricket Club 36, 37, 48
Kensington Oval 33, 60
Kensington Oval Citizens' Improvement Committee 33
King's College 1
Kyffin Thomas, Geoffrey 26–27

L
lacrosse 29–30, 33, 34–35, 53
  Canadian tour of Australia 35
  Interstate Carnival 35
  matches for Australian soldiers, Egypt 36
Lady Gowrie. See Hore-Ruthven, Lady Zara
Lady Victoria Buxton's Girls' Club 68
Lapthorne, William 27–28, 88
Larwood, Harold 39
Laurie, J.B. 19–20, 21
Laverton 27
League of Nations Union 68
Lee, Arthur 27–28, 88
Leonard, A.D.R. 10
Leonora 27
Levinge, Mrs R. 97
Liberal and Country League (LCL) 64
Lichfield (also Carlshurst) 21, *21*, 22, *22*, 24, 50, *51*, 64, 68, *68*, 71, 78, 86, 94, 97
Lindrum, Walter 78
Loloma Gold Mine, Fiji 90, 100
Longson, Edward 19

Lord Gowrie. See Hore-Ruthven, Sir Alexander
Lord Mayor's Patriotic Fund 18
Loreto Convent 66
Lyceum Club 78
Lyons, Jack 37

M
Mailey, Arthur 32
Maitland 66
Manly Golf Club 31
Martindale Hall 52
Marylebone Cricket Club ('MCC') 38, 74
Masson, W.J. 58
McCabe, Stan 31
McCarron, Eddie 42
Melba Theatre 66
Melrose, Alexander 23, 87–88, 90, 99, 100, 110, 123
Melrose Estate 97, 111
Melrose, George 88
Menzies 27
Menzies Government 88
Menzies, Robert Gordon 64
Mick Simmons Ltd 45
Middleton, Roy 31, 32, 39
Miller, Detective Sergeant Ernest 117
Mission to Seamen 68
Miss Lillie Thompson's School 6
Miss Martin's School for Girls 6–7
Morphett, George 71
Mortlock, Mary 5
Mortlock, William Ransom 5

Mount Gambier 66
Mount Magnet 81
Mount Osmond Golf Club 44
Murray, Sir George 73

N
Naracoorte 66
Neill, Mr and Mrs H.N. 23
Neill, Mr H.N. 87, 100
Nelligan, J.W. 103, 105, 123
Newland, Victor 71
Norman, William Ashley 93, 98, 99
North Broken Hill Mining Company 24, 25, 99
Nutter Thomas, Right Rev. Dr Arthur 72, 73

O
Old College School 10
Oxlade, Aubrey 31, 32, 40

P
Packham, Detective 97
Padman, Thomas 16
Paine, Justice Herbert 99, 110
Palais Royal 74, 78
Peacock, Miss L.A.E. 97
Pellew, L.V. 63
Pembroke School 1, 2
philanthropists
 Barr Smith, Robert 52
 Bonython, Sir Langdon 52
 Elder, Sir Thomas 52
 Hughes, Sir Walter 52

Index

Mortlock, John Andrew Tennant 52
Waite, Peter 52
Phillips, E. 101, 102
Phillips, Tom 114, 115
Playford Government 107
Playford, Thomas 96, 106
Police Court 98, 102
Political Reform League 63
Poole, Dorothea 56
Poole, Justice Thomas 72
Port Adelaide Football Club 66
Prince Alfred College 10, 22, 66, 73
Prince George 68
Proud, Cornelius 63

R
radio station 2 UE 45
Reid, Hugh Wesley 97, 103
Reinecke, Carl 21
Richards, Justice Frederick 2, 71, 76, 102, *102*, 103, 105
Richardson, Arthur 23, 97, 111
Richardson, Victor 49
Ridgway, Mark 58
Roberts, Jimmie 19
Robertson, Allen 39, 40
rowing
  Murray Bridge VIII ('The Cods') 34
Royal Adelaide Golf Club 115
Royal Institute for the Blind 65, *65*, 66–67, 88, 91, 102, 103, 111

S
Sands & McDougall 24, 90
Sanford, Sir Wallace 87
Scrymgour, Bernard 39
sharebrokers 2, 23, 26, 86, 97, 106–107, 108
shares 15, 16, 18, 20, 23, 25, 26, 57, 58, 69, 81, 82, 83, 88, 90, 91, 99, 100, 102, 110, 111, 122, 123
Sheffield Shield 37, 38, 42, 43, 49
Simpson Newland, Sir Henry 71
Sir John Melrose Memorial Fund 67
Smith, F.V., KC 98–99, 100
Smith, James 57
Smith (nee Thompson), Lillie 6, 57
Smith, Maurice 27, 88
South Africa (cricket team) 41
South Australian Brewing Company 24, 102
South Australian Brush Company 24, 90, 100
South Australian Cricket Association ('SACA') 37, 42, 43, 44, 47, 48, 51, 74
South Australian Hardcourt Tennis Association 33
South Australian Lacrosse Association 35, 36
South Australian Lawn Tennis Association 33–34
South Australian Police Force 97
Southern Cross 27
speculation, 18, 84, 85, 122
Starr-Bowkett Society 82

St Corantyn 79
St Mark's College 55, *55*, 63, 65, 68, 72
  founding of 54–56
St Mary's Mission of Hope 68
stockbrokers 22, 23, 41, 44, 47, 57, 63, 73, 94
Stock Exchange. See The Stock Exchange of Adelaide
Stock Exchange Patriotic Concert 67
stocks 15, 18, 20, 26
St Peter's College 5, 6, 10–11, *10*, 12, 22, 23, 31, 54, 55, 66, 67, 73
St Peter's Old Collegians' Association 67
Strangway, Detective 97
Sunter, Gordon 57, 61, 89
Supreme Court 11, 102
syndicates 18, 27, 81
  Darwin Hotels 27–28, 88, 123

T
tennis 19, 33
Tester, John 23
T. Hall and Son 81, 83
The Stock Exchange of Adelaide
  and Boer War 19
  call room 15, *16–17*, 17, 29
  Exchange Committee 20, 89, 93, 112, 113, 115
  loyalty to the British Empire 19
  McHenry Street building 15, 17
  Stock Exchange Club 18
  Stock Exchange Rifle Club 18, 33

T.J. Richards & Sons 24, 99
Tobin, J.R. 97
Toc H 53, 68, 78
Travers, Joe 42, 49

U
Union Bank 85, 87, 91, 92, 97, 99, 108, 110
University of Adelaide 6, 52, 54, 72

V
Viner Smith, Cuthbert 89, 93, 95, 96

W
Walkley, Arthur 19
Wasleys 66
Wayville Showgrounds 66
West Australian gold mines
  Coolgardie 27
  Kalgoorlie 19, 27, 117
  Laverton 27
  Leonora 27
  Menzies 27
  Southern Cross 27
Westbrook, Percy 44
Wharton, J.C. 16
wheat futures 84, 85, 86, 123
White, Roy 36
William Sykes Limited 45, 61
Woodfull, Bill 39
Woodlands Church of England Girls' Grammar School 66
Woolworths 24, 102

Y
Yardley, Norman 46
Yatala Labour Prison 2, 105, 116, *116*, 117
Yates, Dorothy 56, 116
Young, Andrew 63, 89, 94, 95, *95*, 109
Yule, Edward 101, 102

Z
Ziesing, George, SM 102
Zinc Corporation Limited 24, 81, 83

Wakefield Press is an independent publishing and
distribution company based in Adelaide, South Australia.
We love good stories and publish beautiful books.
To see our full range of books, please visit our website at
www.wakefieldpress.com.au
where all titles are available for purchase.
To keep up with our latest releases, news and events,
subscribe to our monthly newsletter.

Find us!

Facebook: www.facebook.com/wakefield.press
Twitter: www.twitter.com/wakefieldpress
Instagram: www.instagram.com/wakefieldpress

www.ingramcontent.com/pod-product-compliance
Lightning Source LLC
Chambersburg PA
CBHW020416230426
43663CB00007BA/1188